THE DURHAM BOOK

KV-194-010

This book has been prepared for the Durham County Council by James Wilson, County Planning Officer.

Cover photograph:
View of Durham City from Flass Vale.

Designed by Gill Humphrys, Durham City.
Printed and Bound by Reed Print and Design,
Washington, Tyne and Wear NE38 9DA.

Copyright © Durham County Council
Hardback: ISBN 0 902178 15 6
Paperback: ISBN 0 902178 16 4

THE DURHAM BOOK

DURHAM
COUNTY
COUNCIL

FOREWORD

The Durham County Council produced its first 'Durham Book' in 1973. Our aim in doing this was to draw on the experience of people who knew the area well to paint a more accurate picture of life in the County than was available in existing guide-books produced outside the area. We were delighted that the result was so well received by visitors and residents alike.

Like any other place, County Durham has had its problems and there have been many of them over the centuries – Viking plunderers, Norman devastation, border raids by the Scots, exploitation by the 'captains of industry' in the Industrial Revolution, the great slump of the 1930s and, in more recent years, the loss of thousands of jobs in its traditional industries.

The Durham Book acknowledged these problems but also revealed the much more attractive face of the County which may come as a surprise to some visitors but not to anyone who lives here or knows Durham – the castles and historic houses, the delightful dales villages, the fascinating museums, the lovely countryside and open moors and the magnificent Norman Cathedral in the City of Durham.

The Durham Book also showed what was being done to deal with the problems which remained – by providing new jobs and replacing dereliction with green fields and farmland. This second Durham Book continues the story.

I am proud to have been a member of Durham County Council during a period when so much has been done to improve the County. I am also very pleased, as its present Chairman, to be able to contribute this foreword.

W. Firby,
Chairman Durham County Council

CONTENTS

ILLUSTRATIONS

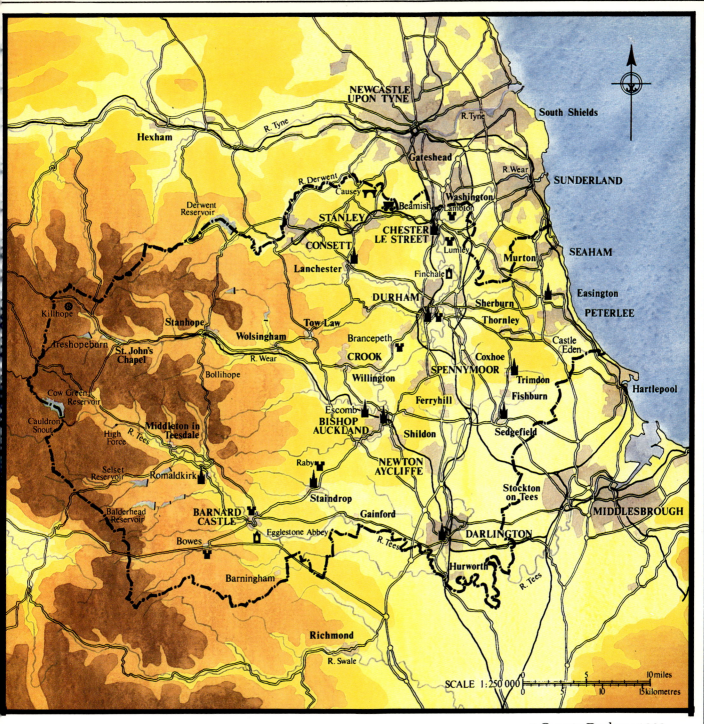

1 County Durham 1982.

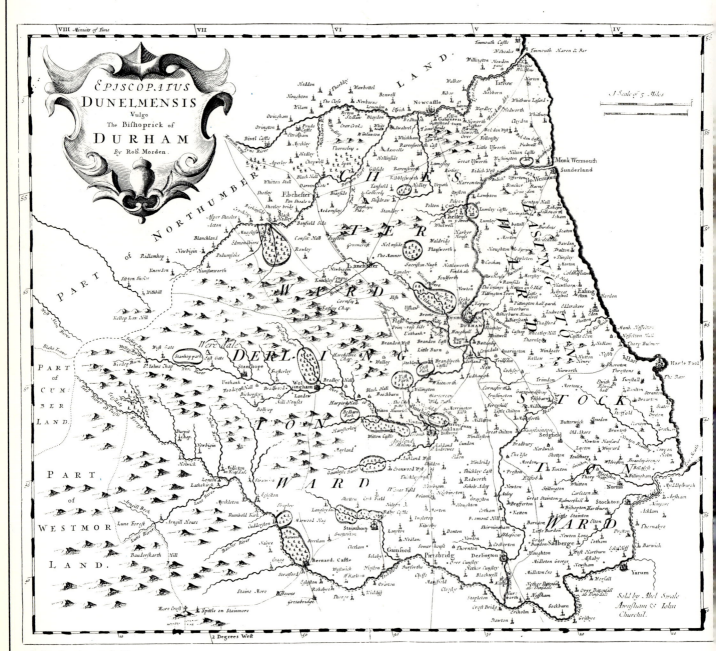

2 Morden's 17th Century
map of the Bishopric of
Durham.

County Durham is one of England's most northerly counties — only 30 miles (50 kilometres) from the Scottish border. For someone travelling the length of Britain – from Brighton on the south coast of England to John O'Groats in the north of Scotland – it is about half-way on the journey.

People who know Durham but have not kept up with government decisions to change county boundaries from time to time would say that the County is the area between the Rivers Tyne and Tees, as indeed it was for many years. That was the original 'Patrimony of St. Cuthbert' in the 9th Century – much as shown on Robert Morden's 17th Century map of the Bishopric of Durham (Plate 2). Since the Bishops of Durham owned land in Yorkshire and Northumberland, it might be said that in historic times the County extended beyond the two rivers but Tyne and Tees were the traditional limits.

In 1974, however, the County's official boundaries were re-drawn. The northern part of Durham, including places like Jarrow, Blaydon and Washington – the home of George Washington's ancestors – became part of a new county based on the Tyne and Wear rivers. A new county of Cleveland also came into being around the mouth of the River Tees to the south, taking in places like Stockton, Billingham and Hartlepool. The new County Durham took in part of the old North Riding of Yorkshire and thereby added a white rose to its coat of arms.

The County has, in effect, moved southwards and become more rural as a result of the 1974 boundary changes. However, its western boundary still runs along the Pennine Hills which form the 'backbone' of Northern England and its eastern boundary is still the North Sea coast, looking across towards southern Denmark and northern Germany. It is also about the same size as before – about 1,000 square miles (2,500 square kilometres). Within its boundaries live 600,000 people.

This book takes account of the changes. The photographs and the map (Plate 1) all relate to the County of Durham as it officially exists today. It is very difficult, however, to write about the County's history without mention of the 'old' Durham. The Boldon Book, the Blaydon Races, the Jarrow March, the shipyards on the River Tyne and the Stockton and Darlington Railway are all firmly embedded in a popular tradition which no amount of local government 'reorganisation' will change.

LANDSCAPE

3 High Force plunging
spectacularly over the
Great Whin Sill.

County Durham covers 1,000 square miles (2,500 square kilometres) within which the landscape ranges from wild, open moorland to rolling farmland and steep, wooded coastal valleys.

In the far west, the land rises to nearly 2,600 feet (790 metres) above sea level on Mickle Fell in the Pennines. The westernmost hills are made of limestone laid down in shallow seas over 300 million years ago. The limestone around Frosterley contains a lot of fossil shells and for this reason has been prized as an ornamental building stone for over seven hundred years.

Earth movements opened up cracks and fissures in the limestone into which flowed hot molten lava from deep below the earth's surface. As the lavas cooled they formed hard bands or 'sills' of basalt, the most famous of which is the Great Whin Sill (Plate 3). The heat of the lava baked the limestone into harder marble in places and, in upper Teesdale, produced the 'sugar limestones' on which grow rare Arctic and Alpine plants. As time passed, natural chemicals in water passing through the rocks combined with the limestone to form new minerals such as lead and fluorspar.

Further to the east, thick bands of sandstone lie on top of the limestone and, above them, peat and heather-clad moors stretch for miles (Plate 4). One can walk freely, enjoying a solitude shared only by sheep and grouse, and breathe really fresh air. As John Speed wrote in 1611:

"The air is sharp and very piercing and would be more, were it not that the vapours from the German seas did much to dissolve her ice and snow."

The ice and snow on the hills usually remain 'undissolved' long enough, however, to look very beautiful and allow skiing in winter (Plate 5).

Three rivers rise in these hills and flow eastwards to the sea; the Tees in the south, where it gushes over some of England's most impressive waterfalls (Plates 3 and 7); the Derwent in the north, which later joins the River Tyne; and, right across the centre of the County, the River Wear. The Tees and the Derwent have been dammed to form large reservoirs (Plate 6).

All three rivers have cut into the moors to create beautiful dales. The pastureland along the sides of the valleys is patterned by stone walls (Plate 8) and stone-built farm houses and cottages (Plate 9). In Teesdale, many of the buildings are white-washed. Small towns and villages shelter in the valley bottoms and the well-wooded lower dales are very beautiful (Plate 10), especially in autumn colours.

New forests have been planted on some of the higher slopes (Plate 11).

As the rivers flow eastwards, they get wider and slower as the level of the land falls. The moorland gives way to lower hills and valleys. In the south of the County, the River Tees flows through a wide plain with gentle slopes and long open views over fields and hedges towards the hills of North Yorkshire (Plate 12). Coal was never worked in this pleasant rural area full of attractive farms and villages.

The River Wear's flow towards the sea changes abruptly at Bishop Auckland where the river swings northwards. To the west of it, the countryside is undulating. Scattered farms with small fields and hedgerows are typical (Plate 13) but occasional patches of wilder, uncultivated fell and common land give the area an ever-changing character. Beneath the land lay the rich coal seams of West Durham.

Around 300 million years ago, the coal seams started life as tangled vegetation in steamy swamps. As the vegetation died, it rotted and was covered by sand. This happened again and again and, as the layers built up, they were gradually compressed into coal and sandstone. Earth movements tilted the rocks so that the coal seams came near to the surface in the west but dipped more deeply beneath other rocks to the east. One quirk of nature led to the preservation of a tree which grew near Edmundbyers over 250 million years ago. Fossilised in a hard stone cast, the tree was brought to Stanhope and is now displayed in the churchyard (Plate 14).

In its northward flow through the centre of the County, the River Wear has created a wide and gently rolling lowland in which are set a number of castles and halls in attractive parkland (Plate 15). The lowlands continue on right up to the River Tyne, into which the Wear once flowed.

In the 'Ice Ages', between two million and 12,000 years ago, great sheets of ice flowing from Scandinavia, Scotland, the Lake District and the Pennines covered all but the highest hills in the County, scouring rocks and soil from the surface. As the glaciers melted and this material was released from the ice, the Wear's flow to the north was blocked and it had to cut itself a new channel from north of Chester le Street to the sea at Sunderland. The valley it had already created to the north has provided an excellent route for the Great North Road, the London to Edinburgh railway and, more recently, the A.1 Motorway. At Ferryhill, the railway runs through a narrow valley carved by water escaping from a huge lake formed by the melting ice.

Between the Wear lowlands and the sea stands a limestone escarpment, running from Pittington in the north to Shildon in the south (Plate 16). The limestones here are different from those in the far west; they are Magnesian limestones and yellow rather than grey (Plate 20). They stand on a thick band of yellow sands which can be seen in quarries on the escarpment. The sands were laid down about 250 million years ago when Durham was a desert and the wind blew the sand into dunes 100 feet (30 metres) high.

On the Magnesian limestones can be found patches of semi-natural grassland and woodland in which grow many rare plants and where the Durham Argus butterfly lives (Plates 17, 18 and 19).

Behind the escarpment the land dips gently down to the sea where the limestone forms buff-coloured cliffs (Plate 21). Streams cutting through the cliffs have cut narrow, steep-sided and very attractive valleys known locally as denes. Castle Eden Dene (Plate 22) is one of the largest of these, penetrating into the heart of the town of Peterlee. The thickly wooded ravine is a natural adventure playground and a shady haven for walking. It is a delightful training ground for naturalists, providing homes for many common and some rare plants, and over 70 species of birds.

The landscape of County Durham is not in its 'natural' state. True, its appearance is strongly influenced by nature's building materials and tools – the rocks and soils and the rivers and the weather. Almost everywhere, however, man has taken a hand in shaping the landscape and the next chapter shows many examples of the buildings and the human activities which have been fitted into the once empty countryside. Before looking at these more obvious examples of man's impact on the County, however, it is worth remarking on his wider influence on the landscape. Only fifty generations ago, much of Durham was an area of forest and woodland with perhaps the hill-tops clear of trees and some patches of boggy land in the lowlands. There were a few clearings in which families scraped a living. The Anglo-Saxons started to clear the forests but large areas survived and, after the arrival of the Normans, were protected for many years as hunting parks for the Bishops. Westgate and Eastgate were the 'gates' of a great deer hunting park in Weardale.

These historic deciduous forests were gradually cut down to provide charcoal for iron-smelting and to build timber ships. Some of the upland forests have been replaced by Forestry Commission conifers at Hamsterley (Plate 23) and in the Stang Forest, right on the County's southern border. Many of the trees in lowland Durham have also been deliberately planted – to shelter farms or to beautify the grounds of the castles and great houses – as at Raby and elsewhere. In very recent years, the County Council has planted many hundreds of thousands of trees to restore spoiled land.

The neat patchwork of fields which we think of as part of the 'unchanging countryside' is, in many places, relatively new. Only three and four hundred years ago, farmers worked in big common fields and lived in villages rather than in farms on their land.

The coming of industry must have made a big impact on the landscape but little evidence of the early days of the Industrial Revolution remains today. You can see where the lead miners washed away the hillsides by 'hushing', but not much else is left to mark their harsh and difficult hours underground (Plate 24). Many of the old quarries in the dales have long been abandoned and now look almost like natural rock outcrops.

Traces of the many pits that dotted the western half of the coalfield are now hard to find. The same goes for the dozens of small ironworks and even the big ones will soon be only a memory. In the minds of many people the County is rightly associated with the hectic years of the Industrial Revolution but its towns and villages never grew big enough to create a vast, grim 'industrial landscape'. With the careful restoration of most of the scars on the landscape, the County cannot complain of a lack of beauty. Indeed, the whole of its western half is of 'outstanding natural beauty' and elsewhere there are many other 'beauty spots'.

4 The heather-clad moors
of West Durham.

7 Cauldron Snout, on the River Tees below Cow Green Reservoir, of which W. H. Auden wrote:
"Always my boy of wish returns
To those peat-stained deserted burns
That feed the WEAR and TYNE and TEES,
And, turning states to strata, sees
How basalt long oppressed broke out
In wild revolt at CAULDRON SNOUT."
New Year Letter 1940.

5 *Top* Upper Teesdale in winter.

6 *Above* Derwent Reservoir, high up on the moors of North West Durham.

8 *Above* Pastureland in Weardale patterned by stone walls.

9 A typical dale farmstead at St. John's Chapel, Weardale.

10 *Above* Beautiful Teesdale as seen from Whistle Crag, near Middleton in Teesdale.

11 Forests on the higher fells. Many conifers have been planted in the last 30 years where once the fells were naturally covered with deciduous trees.

12 Agricultural land on the Tees Plain near Houghton le Side.

13 *Above* Scattered farms with small fields and hedgerows near Satley in North West Durham.

14 The 'fossil tree' at Stanhope.

15 Parkland at Brancepeth, in which is situated one of the County's finest golf courses.

16 The Magnesian Limestone Escarpment near Heugh Hill Hall, Bowburn, East Durham.

17 *Far left* Dark Red Helleborine *(Epipactis Atrorubens).*

18 *Above middle* Durham Argus Butterfly.

19 *Above* The Bird's-eye Primrose *(Primula Farinosa).*

20 *Left* A disused Magnesian Limestone quarry at Pittington Hill.

21 The cliffs near Seaham Hall.

22 *Opposite* Castle Eden Dene – formerly part of the grounds of Castle Eden Hall. Here, Rowland Burdon, the younger, created at the end of the 18th Century a dramatic garden with bridges spanning the ravine and rock pools.

23 The forest at
Hamsterley where the
Forestry Commission
welcome visitors into the
heart of their 5,500 acres
(2,200 hectares). Amidst
the towering conifers
there are picnic sites
beside a stream, nature
trails and a forest drive.

24 The remains of lead
mining in Teesdale – the
Red Grooves Hush above
Newbiggin.

HISTORY
Early Days

25 A 12th Century wall
painting of a bishop
in the Galilee Chapel
of Durham Cathedral.

People have lived in the hills and valleys between the River Tyne and the River Tees for thousands of years – long before the area became known as County Durham. Of those who lived here before the Romans came, saw and conquered, we know little. The tools of Stone Age fishermen are occasionally found along the coast. Stone arrowheads and axeheads tell us that people travelled regularly through Weardale at the end of the Stone Ages, about 4,000 years ago. Later immigrants from across the North Sea – known as the 'Beaker' people from the shape of the pots they made – left pottery fragments at Brandon and Sacriston.

Tools and weapons of bronze found in Heathery Burn Cave, near Stanhope and now displayed in the British Museum show that some of Britain's earliest metal-workers lived in the Durham dales around seven hundred years before the birth of Jesus Christ. There is no such evidence in the County of the people who brought iron working into Britain a few centuries later. Perhaps only a few such families ventured so far north or, perhaps, farming was so much more difficult in the chancier northern climate that people were not settled enough to leave many traces.

THE ROMANS

By the time the Romans arrived in Britain in 43 A.D., Durham was part of the territory of one of the northern Brigantian tribes, possibly centred on Stanwick in North Yorkshire.

The Romans first settled in southern Britain and for some years ignored the north. Relations between the Brigantes and their Roman neighbours blew hot and cold until the Roman Governor Agricola finally conquered the northern tribes in about 80 A.D. The Roman road, later to be known as Dere Street, was built northwards from York to the Firth of Forth in Scotland and along it forts were built at each of the main river crossings in Durham – Piercebridge (Morbio) on the Tees, Binchester (Vinovia) on the Wear, and Ebchester (Vindomora) on the Derwent – and also at Lanchester (Longovicium). Binchester and the River Wear (Vedra) are both mentioned in Ptolemy's geography of the whole known world, published in the Second Century A.D.

The Roman route from Scotch Corner to the west over Stainmore also passed through the County with forts at Greta Bridge (Maglona) and Bowes (Lavatrae) and signal stations further west. There was also a small fortlet at Rey Cross, close to the County boundary with Cumbria. To the east of Dere Street the route from the Humber to the bridge over the Tyne at Newcastle passed through Chester le Street (Concangium) before branching north-eastwards to the Roman port at South Shields.

Small civilian communities gathered around the forts. Aqueducts, bath houses, central heating systems, lime-kilns and one of the most northerly villa estates known in the Roman world (Old Durham, near Durham City) testify to Roman civilisation in the area, as do the ornaments and coins in the impressive Roman collection in The Bowes Museum near Barnard Castle (Plate 26). Essentially, however, Durham remained a frontier district of the Roman Empire only a short distance south of the Emperor Hadrian's famous wall from the Tyne to the Solway and, by 410 A.D., the Romans had gone completely and the way was open for the next wave of invaders.

THE ANGLO-SAXONS

Angles and Saxons from Denmark and Northern Germany settled on the Northumberland Coast and in the Tyne Valley during the 5th and 6th Centuries. Simeon of Durham, in his writings about the 6th Century, tells us that the land between the Tyne and Tees was, at that time, 'a deserted waste ... nothing but a hiding place for wild and woodland beasts'. By the end of the 6th Century, however, it was part of the King Aethelfrith's Kingdom of Northumbria. The northern half of this – Bernicia – most probably covered Northumberland and Durham and the southern half – Deira – most of Yorkshire.

The 7th and 8th Centuries saw the Angles or 'English' establishing villages – in places like Wolsingham, Cleatlam, Easington, Darlington and Hunwick – and taming some of Simeon's 'deserted waste'. The pagan invaders were themselves tamed by Christian missionaries. Paulinus from Kent baptised King Edwin of Northumbria in 627 and eight years later King Oswald invited Aidan to leave the Celtic Christian settlement on Iona and establish a monastic community on the island of Lindisfarne, off the Northumberland coast. One of his successors as Bishop of Lindisfarne, the Anglian Cuthbert, brought to an end the conflict between the Roman and Celtic traditions of Christianity. In this period literature and art blossomed in North East England.

Benedictine monasteries at Monkwearmouth and Jarrow were founded by Benedict Biscop at the end of the 7th Century. The 'father of English history' – the Venerable Bede – lived all his life from the age of seven in these two monasteries and produced his Ecclesiastical History of the English Speaking People. Plates 27 and 28 show the Church of St. John the Evangelist at Escomb, which has miraculously survived from the times of Bede, having been built with Roman masonry from the nearby fort at Binchester (Vinovia). There are examples in Durham Cathedral of the sculpture of this period (Plate 29).

THE VIKINGS

Viking raids from Denmark at the end of the 8th Century shattered this peaceful world. Buildings were looted and burned and organised monastic life destroyed. The English held out north of the Tees for a time and the Scandinavians settled mainly in the south of the County as local place names of Norse origin show – Sadberge, Raby, Killerby, Selaby. The Vikings harassed the Lindisfarne community until they left their home and began seven years of wandering with the body of St. Cuthbert. Eventually, in 883, they settled at Chester le Street and built a church on the site of the present parish church (Plate 30). Although it is difficult to understand why, the Scandinavian rulers of Yorkshire actually ratified the rights of St. Cuthbert's followers over the lands between the Tyne and the Tees and, with this decision, we see the origins of the 'County of Durham' – just over 1,000 years ago.

The trials and tribulations of the Community of St. Cuthbert were not over, however. They were later driven from Chester le Street as far south as Ripon in Yorkshire and we are told that, on the way back, Cuthbert's coffin became fixed to the ground and the monks were bidden in a vision to take it to Dunholm (the 'hill island'). They followed a girl looking for her dun cow (commemorated in a Cathedral carving – Plate 31) to find the naturally defended Durham peninsula. Here a shrine was built for Cuthbert's body with the help of the Northern ruler Uhtred who brought in workers to build a stone church. To this shrine, known as the White Church, were later brought the bones of Bede from Jarrow. It was an important place of pilgrimage and among its visitors was King Canute.

THE NORMANS

Following the Norman invasion of 1066, the Northern English rebelled against William the Conqueror, who retaliated with the devastation and massacre known as the 'harrying of the North'. He appointed Walcher as Bishop of Durham in 1071, seeking to make use of the religious power and prestige of Cuthbert's bishopric in order to secure a greater measure of civil control in the area. Walcher was also made Earl of Northumberland with complete jurisdiction between the Tees and the Scottish border.

William the Conqueror and his successor William Rufus gave land to other faithful retainers. The Count of Brittany was made Earl of Richmond for his efforts at the Battle of Hastings and he marked his territory by building a castle at Bowes on the site of the Roman fort; this castle was later replaced by one built for Henry II. Guy de Baliol was given land in Teesdale where his son Bernard built the castle after which the town of Barnard Castle was named. Both castles are now picturesque ruins (Plates 32 and 33).

The powers of the Bishops of Durham were so extensive that even the Domesday Survey stopped short of the County boundary. They had their own armies, coined their own money, owned all the mines and were more like the Prince-Bishops of Germany than English Bishops (Plate 25). Whatever the King could do outside the County, the Bishop could do inside!

Bishops with such powers needed a castle rather than a palace and Bishop Walcher started to build his castle on the steep rock in Durham around which the River Wear loops (Plate 34). It was an easy site to defend and the castle was strong enough to repel Danish attacks in 1075. It is one of the most impressive and best preserved Norman castles in the country. Owned by the University, its Norman Chapel (Plate 35) and Gallery and the 13th Century Great Hall are open to the public.

Bishop Walcher's successor, William de St. Carileph made a lasting impact with his particular building project – the magnificent Durham Cathedral (Plates 36 and 37). Having seen many new churches in Normandy during temporary exile there, he destroyed the Saxon church in 1092 and the following year started to build the present Cathedral. Most of the building was completed within 40 years. Today, the view of Durham Cathedral, together with its monastery and nearby castle is, according to the noted architectural historian Professor Pevsner, one of the great architectural experiences of Europe, comparable only with Prague and Avignon.

26 *Right* Part of the collection of Roman coins and ornaments held at The Bowes Museum. Most were found at the fort of Binchester *(Vinovia)*, near Bishop Auckland.

27 *Below* Church of St. John the Evangelist, Escomb. Dating from the 7th Century, it is the least altered Anglo-Saxon church in the North of England.

28 *Left* Interior of the church of St. John the Evangelist, Escomb, looking down the tall, narrow nave towards the altar on which rests a small Saxon cross.

29 *Below* An 11th Century cross head which was built into the foundations of the Chapter House of Durham Cathedral, probably as a memorial to the Community of St. Cuthbert.

30 Church of St. Mary and St. Cuthbert, Chester le Street, built on the site of the church founded by the Community of St. Cuthbert after their arrival in 883. Eardulph, the 16th Bishop of Lindisfarne, became the first Bishop of Chester le Street and gifts of land and privileges were bestowed on this new bishopric by the Scandinavian rulers of Yorkshire. The present church dates from the 13th Century.

31 The carving on Durham Cathedral commemorating the legend that the monks carrying St. Cuthbert's coffin were guided to Durham by a milk maid looking for her dun cow.

33

32 Bowes Castle was built for Henry II near to the site of the Roman fort of *Lavatrae*.

33 The spectacular ruins of Barnard Castle built in the 12th Century by Bernard Baliol whose father, Guy de Baliol, came to Britain from Bailleul in Picardy during the Norman Conquest.

34 The peninsula of
Durham City on which was
built the Cathedral and Castle,
defended on three sides by
the steep gorge of the River
Wear.

35 The sculptured capitals of the Norman Chapel in Durham Castle.

36 Durham Cathedral –
view from Prebends'
Bridge. A plaque on the
bridge quotes the lines of
Sir Walter Scott:
"Grey towers of Durham
Yet well I love thy mixed
    and massive piles
Half church of God, half
    castle 'gainst the Scot".

HISTORY
The Middle Ages

37 Interior of Durham
Cathedral, looking down
the chancel and nave from
the High Altar and
showing the massive piers
and the famous rib
vaulting – the earliest of its
kind in Western Europe.

The Prince-Bishops of Durham continued to flourish during the Middle Ages. Bishop Hugh de Puiset (Pudsey) amassed great wealth and some of his possessions, including his beautifully illuminated bible, are among the silver plate and other church furnishings now on display in the Cathedral Treasury (Plates 38 and 41). Other exhibits include the 7th Century cross from St. Cuthbert's coffin (Plate 40), the remains of the coffin itself and Bishop Hatfield's seal (Plate 39).

In 1189, Bishop de Puiset added to the bishopric the Wapentake of Sadberge, a tract of land on the north bank of the Tees and thus first created County Durham as it later existed. Sadberge has, however, maintained its distinction as a royal manor and earldom. A stone can still be seen on the village green commemorating Queen Victoria's Jubilee and inscribed to 'Victoria, Queen of the United Kingdom, Empress of India and Countess of Sadberge.'

In order to keep a check on his lands, de Puiset carried out his own 'Domesday Survey' of the County. The results are contained in the Boldon Book – so called because Boldon was the first place in it. The survey tells us something about the estate reorganisation and agricultural development in the County after the earlier devastation. Many of the 'green' villages of the County – farms and cottages fronting onto an open common or green – date from this period. Much of the farming was pastoral in nature but corn was grown around Darlington and there were forests in the west. It does not sound too different from today! Most people had to carry out services for the Bishops – fencing, carrying, helping with the hunts and even mining. Mineral exploitation in the bishopric took place mainly in the west – Bishop de Puiset had royal permission to mine silver and lead in Weardale. Iron ore was also mined in the west where it was smelted and forged with charcoal, even though coal was already being worked.

The records of all this activity do not give us the names of individual miners and farmers but the names and exploits of their lords are described in detail. Members of two local families actually became kings of Scotland – Robert de Brus of Hartlepool and John de Baliol of Barnard Castle. Others influenced English history – particularly the Nevilles of Raby and Brancepeth. The tomb of Ralph Neville (Plate 42) can be found in Staindrop Church (Plate 43). Ralph Neville beat the Scots at Nevilles Cross in 1346 and the family later became

Earls of Westmorland. They were deeply involved in Plantagenet politics during the Wars of the Roses when Cecily 'the Rose of Raby' married the Duke of York and was mother of Edward IV and Richard III. They eventually fell from power after choosing to support Mary Queen of Scots in the Rising of the North against Elizabeth I. The Baron's Hall where this ill-fated plot was hatched was later poetically described by Wordsworth:

"Seven hundred knights, retainers all of Neville, at their master's call had sate together at Raby's Hall."

Raby Castle, set in beautiful parkland, is now open to the public (Plate 44). As well as seeing the Baron's Hall, one can wander through sumptuous state rooms containing fine period furniture and paintings (Plate 45). Outside, a collection of horse-drawn carriages is housed in the Palladian stables. The Nevilles' other castle at Brancepeth also still stands but much of what can be seen today, including the 'chessmen' gate-towers, is a 19th Century imitation, commissioned by a wealthy family of coal owners (Plate 46).

Other great families were the Lumleys, the Hyltons and the Eures. Licences to fortify their castles at Lumley, Hylton and Witton le Wear were issued in the 14th and 15th Centuries. Lumley is still an impressive, square-towered, late 14th Century building (Plate 47) with a few later alterations by Sir John Vanbrugh. The castle is at present used as an hotel but is still in the ownership of the Lumleys, now Earls of Scarborough.

Witton Castle, once the home of the Eure family, is today owned by the Lambtons, whose Lambton Castle is really another 19th Century romantic creation (Plate 48). Lambton Castle is on the site of the home of John Lambton, who killed the 'Lambton Worm', a legendary serpent which terrorised the neighbourhood, and of John George Lambton, first Earl of Durham and High Commissioner and Governor General of Canada in the 1830s. The 'Greek Doric' temple erected as a monument to him at nearby Penshaw can be seen from all over the north of the County.

Less well-known families built manor houses on a more modest scale, including the recently restored East Deanery, once the home of the Dean of St. Andrew Auckland; Stanhope Hall; Crook Hall in Durham City (Plate 49); and Witton Tower, originally a defended 'pele' tower.

Noble families were not the only builders, however. Successive bishops left their mark in the form of fine churches, bridges and hospitals. Bishop Flambard founded Kepier Hospital in Durham and built the City walls and Framwellgate Bridge (Plate 50). Bishop de Puiset founded Sherburn Hospital (Plate 51) and constructed Elvet Bridge and St. Cuthbert's church in Darlington – one of the most important Early English churches in the North of England (Plate 52). He also started to build a new palace at Bishop Auckland (Plate 53). Set in parkland and complete with a Gothic cloister to shelter the deer (Plate 54), it is now the permanent residence of the Bishops of Durham.

The County's two ruined monastic buildings also date from this period. The hermit and former pirate, St. Godric, settled at Finchale in 1115, later the site of Finchale Priory (Plate 56). A peaceful riverside setting was also chosen for the abbey at Egglestone (Plate 55), which was painted by Turner and eulogized by Sir Walter Scott.

Ecclesiastical influence can also be seen in place names up and down the County – Bishop Middleham, Bishopton, Sacriston and Bearpark (from beau repaire, the 'beautiful retreat' of the Prior of Durham). Other village names remind us of the Norman influence – Beamish (Bewmys) and Butterby (Beutroue) are old French names mangled by English mouths – or of once prominent local lords – Witton Gilbert, Hutton Henry and Coatham Mundeville.

Slowly, the towns began to grow. Licences were granted to hold markets in Durham City, Darlington, Sedgefield, Staindrop, Wolsingham and Barnard Castle where Blagraves, a fine early town house, still survives. Durham City, which was granted its charter in 1180, Darlington and Bishop Auckland gradually emerged as the major centres, but they still remained small towns partly, perhaps, due to the fact that the Bishops feared any municipal challenge to their authority.

Their growth may also have been kept in check by constant border warfare. Having been earlier devastated by William the Conqueror, who 'left not a house standing between York and Durham', the County was laid waste by King David I of Scotland who put his own nominee in the Bishop's palace in 1140. The Scots again invaded in 1217; were stopped on the Tyne in 1297 with, reputedly, the assistance of St. Cuthbert's spirit; were bought off dearly at the start of the 14th Century; but attacked again in force practically every decade up to the Battle of Nevilles Cross in 1346. Forty years later they were back again to plunder. What with crop failures, plagues and famines, it is little wonder that there was economic and population decline. Villages disappeared, social unrest and lawlessness prevailed and, although many criminals were caught and dealt with at the Palatinate's own court, others claimed sanctuary by clasping the Cathedral knocker (Plate 57).

In 1536, Henry VIII took over from the Bishops the responsibility for justice in Durham and this and other acts of 'centralisation' may well have helped to provoke the northern Catholic rebellion, known as the Pilgrimage of Grace, supported by members of all the Durham noble families except Sir William Eure. After the rebellion petered out, St. Cuthbert's shrine was despoiled and the Durham monks were dispersed. The similar Rising of the North in 1569 also collapsed.

cum nigli siiii in coniuro. & iohs filu sy
monis occidit eosq ueniam pderc eum

EXPLICIVNT: CAPITVLA :·
INCIPIT : LIBER : PRIMVS
MACHABEORVM :·

darui

regnauit in grecia. egressus de terra
cechim darij regem psarum & medo
constituit plia multa. & omium ob
nuit munitiones. Et interfecit rege
terre. & ptransiit usqz ad fines terre.

39 Bishop Hatfield's 14th Century seal, illustrating the secular powers of the Bishops.

40 *Above* The 7th Century Pectoral Cross taken from St. Cuthbert's coffin in 1827.

8 *Opposite* A capital letter from Hugh de Puiset's (Bishop Pudsey) illuminated bible (12th century).

41 Silver plate from the time of Bishop Cosin (17th Century).

42 Stone figures on the tomb of Ralph Neville, 1st Earl of Westmorland, in Staindrop Church. His 'companions' are his two wives, Joan Beaufort, daughter of John of Gaunt and sister of Henry IV, and Margaret, daughter of the Earl of Stafford.

43 Staindrop Church, dating from the 12th Century.

44 Raby Castle, fortified in the 14th Century, is one of the most impressive castles in the North of England.

45 The interior of Raby Castle. The Baron's Hall where the Lord of Raby assembled his seven hundred knights; the scene of the ill-fated plot to rise up against Elizabeth I in support of Mary Queen of Scots and the church of Rome.

46 *Left* Brancepeth Castle was originally a mediaeval castle owned by the Neville family but most of the present castle was built in the 19th Century. William Russell, a banker and financier from Sunderland who made his fortune from the coal industry, bought the castle for £75,000 in 1796. His son Matthew commissioned the extensive alterations.

47 *Below* Lumley Castle, built in the 14th Century by Sir Ralph Lumley. In 1580, John Lord Lumley decorated the gatehouses with heraldic shields, erected an equestrian statue to his legendary Saxon ancestor Liulph, and placed a row of tombs (some genuine but several false) in Chester le Street parish church.

48 *Left* Lambton Castle, a 19th Century romantic creation of towers and buttresses set in a park of over 2,000 acres (800 hectares).

49 Crook Hall in Durham City is the most complete mediaeval manor house in the County.

50 *Opposite above* ▶ Framwellgate Bridge in Durham City, built in 1120 by Bishop Flambard.

51 *Opposite below* ▶ Sherburn Hospital, near Durham City, founded by Bishop de Puiset in 1181 as a leper hospital dedicated to 'Christ, the Blessed Virgin Mary, Lazarus and his sisters Martha and Mary'. In 1434, Bishop Langley refounded the hospital as an almshouse.

52 St. Cuthbert's Church, Darlington, was started in 1192 on the orders of Bishop de Puiset and became an important church in the Durham Diocese. The spire is a landmark in the town.

53 The Bishop's Palace at Bishop Auckland dates from the 12th Century when it was built as a residence for Bishop de Puiset. Following the gift of Durham Castle to Durham University by Bishop Van Mildert, Auckland Palace became the permanent home of all succeeding bishops.

54 *Above* Gothic deer-shelter in Auckland Park, complete with turrets and a tower which once contained a banqueting hall.

55 Egglestone Abbey, near Barnard Castle, founded at the end of the 12th Century.

57 The great sanctuary
knocker of the Cathedral.
Any fugitives who
clutched the knocker were
granted admittance to the
Cathedral. If, after 37 days
they had not settled their
affairs, they were given
safe conduct to the coast
and out of the realm.

56 *Opposite* Finchale
Priory, a 13th Century
retreat for the monks of
Durham. The ruins can be
found in a delightful
setting on the wooded
banks of the River Wear.

HISTORY
The 17th to
19th Centuries

58 The Market Cross at
Barnard Castle, an
octagonal building of
1747. Originally the
market traders sold their
wares beneath the
colonnade, whilst the
council and court met in
the chamber above.

In these more settled times, and helped by demand from a growing population of miners, a lot was done to improve farming and increase food production. The huge, open common fields were gradually split into smaller plots by walls and fences. The centuries-old 'infield – outfield' system – more like Scottish than English farming – was replaced by more productive methods. The evidence of enclosure can be very clearly seen around Lanchester, with straight roads, large fields and dry-stone walls (Plate 59). There was a growth in skills and understanding which led to innovation. A Durham company manufactured table mustard for the first time and made this new and exciting condiment nationally famous (Plate 60). Years of breeding shorthorn cattle for the production of meat and of fat for soap and candle-making led to the Durham Ox, a famous specimen raised by the Colling brothers at Ketton, near Darlington (Plate 61). Exhibited throughout the country, it weighed nearly a ton and a half. Sheep breeds were also improved to provide more meat and wool. At the same time craft industries prospered, including linen-making on the Tees.

Farming families became wealthier and the richer ones built themselves handsome country houses, many of which still adorn the County. Amongst them are Quarry Hill House, a Tudor house near Brancepeth (Plate 64), and Gainford Hall, a Jacobean mansion (Plate 63). Horden Hall, of the same period (Plate 62), was built by the Conyers family and West Auckland Hall was the home of the Edens. This latter local family was to produce a Governor-General of India, the Earl of Auckland after whom Auckland in New Zealand was named, and a Prime Minister – Sir Anthony Eden.

Other fine 17th Century houses are Westernhopeburn in Weardale (Plate 66), Westholme near Winston, Unthank Hall at Stanhope and, near Wolsingham, Bishop Oak Hall with its charming gazebo (Plate 65). In Wolsingham itself are Whitfield Place (Plate 67) and Whitfield House. The more humble dwellings of this period have long since disappeared.

Along with the development of farming went the growth of the mining industry. Silver and lead had been worked in the west certainly from the Middle Ages and probably far earlier. Coal was also mined in the 13th and 14th Centuries and transported by sea to distant markets. Queen Elizabeth I sought to persuade the Bishop of the time to put mining in the hands of a consortium of businessmen known as the 'Grand Lease'. The industry provided not only jobs for miners but fortunes and honours for these 'coal owners'. Rivalries between them grew to the extent that Tyneside and Wearside took different sides in the Civil War. The mining of coal and its transport, first to the river estuaries and then by sea to southern markets, stimulated ship and wagonway building so that, by the end of the 17th Century, coalmining had become a very advanced and highly integrated industrial enterprise.

The arrival of the new breed of businessmen was marked by political changes. Although some of the old noble families, like the Nevilles, had already been replaced by newer ones – such as the Vanes – the old traditions had not changed much. However, some of the new merchant families – like the Lilburnes – had an interest in more radical changes. Robert Lilburne, Squire of Thickley, was one of Cromwell's colleagues and, for a time, commander-in-chief in Scotland. He was one of those who signed Charles I's death warrant. His brother, John Lilburne was the leader of the 'Levellers' – a group of people with intense belief in religious and social equality.

The restoration of the monarchy after Cromwell's death saw a return to strong episcopal influence in the County with pro-royalist Bishops like Cosin and Crewe. Cosin did a lot of restoration work in the County's churches, leaving us some marvellously carved woodwork (Plates 68 and 69). It was not until after his death, however, that Durham was allowed to send Members of Parliament to the House of Commons – two for the County and two for the City. Previously, there had been parliamentary representation only during Cromwell's protectorate, or by way of the Bishop's seat in the House of Lords. Amongst the County's early M.P.s was 'Bonny Bobby Shafto' of Whitworth Hall, whose election song became a popular nursery rhyme.

Bishop Crewe was, perhaps, more of a reactionary than some of his predecessors and, in a rapidly changing world, brought his office into considerable disrepute by several ill-judged actions, including support for and later repudiation of King James II. The Church consequently played less and less of a part in the affairs of the County and the names of families like Vane, Tempest and Lambton appeared more frequently in its chronicles.

The new squirearchy built themselves elegant houses: Freville Lambton built the dignified

Biddick Hall (Plate 71) which Sir John Vanbrugh may have influenced and, a little later, Elemore Hall near Pittington was built in the Palladian style. Elemore Hall, like Auckland Palace, Croxdale Hall and St. Helen Hall, contains marvellous plaster-work done by talented Italian craftsmen who obviously travelled from job to job as one landowner after another sought to be 'in fashion' (Plates 70 and 72).

Many pleasant Georgian country houses have survived from the 18th Century including those at Hurworth (Plate 74), Beamish (Plate 75) and Castle Eden. Hamsterley Hall is a charming example of Georgian 'gothick' with its pinnacle from the old Houses of Parliament (Plate 73). In the early 19th Century, before Queen Victoria gave her name to a 64 year span of industrial growth, designs were more classical as seen in the work of the architect Ignatius Bonomi who designed Burn Hall and Eggleston Hall.

Increasing prosperity spread its influence in both towns and villages until it was not only the landed gentry who had fashionable houses. Using local materials and the skills of local craftsmen, many simple but attractive houses were built around the village greens. Examples can be found in many places including Barningham (Plate 76) and Romaldkirk (Plate 77) where they cluster around the 12th Century 'kirk' (church) of St. Romuald, the son of a Northumbrian king. Similarly, further down Teesdale, Gainford and Hurworth (Plate 78) contain fine 18th and 19th Century houses.

Of the towns in the County, Durham City and Barnard Castle contain the best collections of town houses from this period. Durham City, dominated by its Cathedral and Castle, has many handsome Georgian town houses (Plates 79 and 80).

Barnard Castle is a lovely country market town with wide streets, a dramatic ruined castle and a fascinating collection of historic buildings dating from the 16th Century. These include weavers' cottages with their attic workshop windows, the Market Cross of 1747 (Plate 58), and a 'French chateau'.

Many other important public and ecclesiastical buildings date from this period. Examples are Ushaw College, near Durham City, and Bishop Auckland's Town Hall, with its curious French character, in the middle of the market place (Plate 81). Here a weekly market takes place, overlooked by 18th and 19th Century town houses.

59 Aerial photographs
provide evidence of past
enclosures near
Lanchester. Between 1781
and 1784, 15,000 acres
(6,000 hectares) of
Lanchester Fell were
enclosed. Out of the
'barren, desert and dreary
common', land was
reclaimed to produce
crops of grain and provide
valuable pastureland.
Allotment boundaries
were drawn with
precision and wide
straight drove roads were
defined by stone walls.

AINSLEY'S
GENUINE DURHAM MUSTARD,

Manufactured and Sold ONLY at the Original Manufactory,

22, FOOT OF SILVER-STREET, DURHAM.

ESTABLISHED 1692.

THE Nobility, Clergy, Gentry, and Inhabitants generally of Durham and its vicinity, are respectfully informed that the above CELE-BRATED MUSTARD is made from the finest selected Samples of English Brown Seed, on the principles which first gave to Durham its celebrity for the Article, combined with every Improvement which science has since developed. The greatest skill and attention is observed in the preparation of the Seed, which is desiccated in a manner known only to the Proprietor of the above Establishment, whereby all its strength, flavour, and piquant qualities are retained. It is warranted to be free from every adulter-ation, such as Turmeric, Horse Raddish, Flour, Pepper, &c., and, to prove it, is at all times open to analyzation.

Sold Wholesale and Retail in Bottles, Bladders and Casks ; and, to protect the Public from being imposed upon, each Label with the Bottles, Bladders, &c., will have upon it a representation of Durham Cathedral and the City Arms, and without which it is not Ainsley's Mustard.

☞ Other Parties of the NAME OF AINSLEY having commenced to Man-ufacture Mustard, it is considered necessary to inform the Public that no person of that name, living in any part of the Town, except at 22, Silver-Street, ever had or has any connexion whatever with the above Old Estab-lished Business.

OBSERVE THE SIGNATURE OF

Jno Balmbrough

22, Foot of Silver-Street, Durham.

60 Mustard – Durham's new and exciting condiment!

61 *Below* The Durham Ox. At five years old he was thought to be 'so wonderful an animal and so far exceeding whatever had been seen before, that he was bought for £140 in 1801 to be exhibited throughout the country' – a no mean task given the problems of transporting a beast of 270 stones.

62 *Far left* Horden Hall, from around 1600, was built by Sir Christopher Conyers. Its fine porch is flanked by Tuscan columns.

63 *Left* Gainford Hall, dated 1603, was built by the Rev. John Cradock.

64 *Left* Quarry Hill House, near Brancepeth, a tall symmetrical house with gabled bays, built in the early 17th Century.

65 The 17th Century gazebo in the garden of Bishop Oak Hall, in Wolsingham.

66 *Opposite above* ▶ Westernhopeburn, a long, low stone house, built in 1606 in Weardale.

67 *Opposite below* ▶ Whitfield Place, Wolsingham, an attractive three bay, two storey house of 1677, has recently been restored.

68 and 69 Bishop Cosin undertook a large scale restoration programme for the County's churches. He is especially noted for his influence upon the fine woodwork which can now be seen in many churches. *Left* Bishop Cosin's font cover in Durham Cathedral which stands 40 feet (12 metres) high, and *below* pews and screens in St. Edmund's Church, Sedgefield.

70 Attractive Rococo plasterwork at Elemore Hall near Pittington.

71 *Above* The handsome proportions of Biddick Hall, residence of the Lambton family.

72 The elegant interior of the Hall at St. Helen Auckland.

73 Hamsterley Hall with its pinnacle from the old Houses of Parliament. This was the home of the Gort family, the most distinguished member of which was Field Marshal Lord Gort – Commander in Chief of the British Expeditionary Force in France.

74 Hurworth Hall, now a private school.

75 Beamish Hall, now part of the North of England Open Air Museum.

76 Late 18th Century houses in the village of Barningham, one of Teesdale's attractive villages.

77 *Above* The village green and 12th Century church at Romaldkirk in Teesdale dedicated to St. Romuald. The village has delightful interconnecting greens and a mixture of stone cottages and large Georgian houses.

78 Victorian gothic cottages along the main street at Hurworth, near Darlington.

79 Georgian town houses in Bow Lane, Durham City.

80 The 18th Century doorcase of Cosin's Hall on Palace Green.

81 The Market Place at
Bishop Auckland, once
crossed by a Roman road,
contains the solemn
Gothic town hall and the
adjacent church of St.
Anne. The scene is
enlivened every week by
the colours and bustle of
the town's popular
market.

HISTORY
The Industrial Revolution

2 Causey Arch is the
orld's oldest surviving
ilway bridge. It was built
1727 by Ralph Wood, a
cal stonemason who,
cording to local
adition, later committed
icide because he was
raid that it might fall
wn.

From being the part-time occupation of many dales farmers, leadmining became an important industry in the hills of Teesdale and Weardale in the 18th Century. New veins of ore were exposed by 'hushing' – washing away the topsoil by suddenly releasing dammed watercourses. The Quaker London Lead Company established a northern headquarters at Middleton in Teesdale (Plates 84 and 85) providing houses, schools and medical facilities in return for sober diligence. The miners suffered a high risk of pneumonia and rheumatism from the harsh climate which added to all the normal risks of mining.

By the middle of the 19th Century, lead dressing – the separation of ore from waste – had been mechanised. New machinery was installed by the Blackett Beaumont Company at their Park Level Mill at Killhope in Weardale (Plate 86). The mill was powered by a great iron water wheel – 34 feet (10 metres) in diameter (Plate 83).

The County is, however, better known for its coal. Coal was first worked in the shallowest seams in the west, often by 'drifts' from the surface where the seams outcropped. Shafts were later sunk to reach the deeper seams and, by 1650, had reached a depth of 400 feet (120 metres) or so. To go deeper needed new techniques to drain and ventilate the mines and, in the early 18th Century, the use of the Newcomen steam engine to pump out the mines was an important milestone.

Once on the surface, the coal had to be transported. At first it was carried in horse-drawn 'chaldron' wagons and later in wagons pulled by huge cables worked by stationary steam engines. The County's landscape was criss-crossed by these wagonways, one of which was carried across the Causey Burn by the world's oldest surviving railway bridge, built in 1727 (Plate 82). Mr. Howitt, a traveller from the South was fascinated by them:

"Here and there, you saw careering over the plain, long trains of coal waggons, without horses or attendants or any apparent cause of motion but their own mad agency. They seemed, indeed, rather driven or dragged by unseen demons."

It was not long before the 'unseen demons' – long wire ropes – were replaced by the steam railway locomotives which, from their birthplace in North East England, were to run all over the world. Three local men dominated early railway history – George Stephenson (Plate 87), Timothy Hackworth (Plate 88) and Edward Pease (Plate 89). Stephenson developed the steam locomotive; Hackworth, a skilled engineer, built and modified engines at the Shildon works; and Pease provided the initiative and cash for the history-making Stockton and Darlington Railway, the first passenger railway in the world.

The new railway opened on 27th September, 1825 (Plates 90 and 92), with the engine – 'Locomotion' – drawing 80 tons of coal, engineers and committee men at between 10 and 12 miles (16 and 19 kilometres) an hour. 'Locomotion' (Plate 91) is now on display in the North Road Museum at Darlington and a replica puffs along the tracks in the North of England Open Air Museum at Beamish. Some of Hackworth's engines can be seen at the Hackworth Museum in Shildon. They include a replica of 'Sanspareil', which was beaten by Stephenson's 'Rocket' in the Rainhill Locomotive Trials in 1829.

Darlington grew and prospered under the influence of these local entrepreneurs – especially the Peases and Backhouses. These two important Quaker families built or bequeathed many fine buildings including the well known clock tower which stands high above the Market Hall (Plate 93). The Friends' Meeting House in Skinnergate is further evidence of Quaker influence in the town. Like Pease's own house (Plate 94), it has been recently restored.

Building the first railways led to more firsts – including the first iron railway bridge (Plate 95), now in the National Railway Museum at York, and the first 'skewed' railway bridge – both built across the River Gaunless near West Auckland. Then came the many magnificent viaducts, like Hounsgill (Plate 96). After being, for many centuries, rather cut-off from what was happening in the rest of the country – deliberately so under some of the Bishops – Durham was at the very centre of the 'new' Britain.

By the middle of the 19th Century, the pace of invention and industrialisation was increasing in the County and, indeed, the whole of North East England was in a ferment. The Region produced the friction match, the first coke by-product plant (at Crook in County Durham), developed iron ships and screw propulsion, built the first tanker, and invented the turbine and the incandescent lamp.

Many of these developments were a direct consequence of the growth of coalmining. To get the coal from the collieries (Plate 98) to its markets, the railways were built and staithes and coal-drops constructed at the coal ports like Seaham Harbour

(Plate 97). Most of the collier-ships were built in the Region and this, in turn, created a demand for iron plates. By 1860 County Durham had 58 ironworks with blast furnaces (Plate 99). The largest of these were at Spennymoor, Darlington, Witton Park, Seaham, Tow Law and Consett – it is little wonder that in the second half of the century, North East England built two out of every five ships in the world. By the turn of the century, Spennymoor was to have the largest plate-mill in Europe and the Consett Iron Works (Plate 100), founded by the Derwent Iron Company in 1839, dominated the area. Iron making in Consett had started much earlier and the arrival of sword-makers from Solingen in Germany in the late 17th Century brought world famous craftsmen to the area.

The railway engines and ships and the iron-works themselves all needed fuel and the demand for coal continued to grow well into the 20th Century when, with the use of new coal-cutting machines (Plate 102) to supplement 'hand-hewing', production from the Durham coalfield reached a peak of over 41 million tons in 1911.

The rapid growth of industry brought prosperity to some in the County, but many problems as well: long hours of work for low pay, death and accidents in the mines and factories, poor and overcrowded houses.

Coalmining was a hard and dirty job and the grim appearance of the pits showed it (Plate 101). Huge heaps of pit waste rose up like a rash on the face of the County, often burning and smoking for years. Railway embankments and cuttings criss-crossed the countryside; quarries gouged deeply into the landscape and the rivers and streams were polluted. Not satisfied with ruining the land, some of the pits tipped their waste into the sea and fouled the beaches (Plate 103).

Like the pits, the workers' houses built by the coal owners were instruments of profit rather than comfortable homes. Small and cramped, they were often laid out in long monotonous rows alongside unmade streets (Plate 104), with earth closets and water from standpipes. The pit heaps or the ironworks loomed above the houses. The whole environment was mechanical and dreary with no shops or playing fields, only perhaps a pub and a 'tin' chapel.

Some Durham mining villages such as Trimdon with its long green and Norman church and Easington, where the Early English church stands prominent, high above the green, did manage to keep more than a trace of their rural beginnings. Many others were, however, redeemed only by the spirit of the people living in them and the green fields around them.

Industrial growth also brought major social changes. The rapidly growing workforce, many of whom came into the County from elsewhere, worshipped in non-conformist chapels rather than in the established Anglican churches. The workers also banded together to try and improve their working conditions and to get rid of such practices as eviction from their colliery-owned houses during strikes. The Durham Miners' Association was formed in 1869 and the fight for rights threw up such workers' champions as Peter Lee, after whom the new town in the east of the County was later named. The strength of the miners' unions was symbolised in the annual Durham Miners' Gala or 'big meeting' when thousands of miners and their families marched into Durham City behind their lodge banners (Plates 105 to 108). Even today, with only a handful of working collieries in the County, it still attracts thousands of visitors.

In the middle of this industrial ferment and among the inventors and entrepreneurs, more artistic talents were being nurtured. Thomas Sheraton the furniture designer lived in Stockton; William Emmerson the mathematician in Hurworth; and Elizabeth Barrett Browning was born at Coxhoe Hall. Robert Surtees the antiquary lived at Mainsforth and Robert Smith Surtees, the author, at Hamsterley in North West Durham. Lord Byron married Isabella Milbanke at Seaham and Wordsworth met his future wife at Sockburn.

The County also inspired the talents of visitors. A house in Bowes was used by Charles Dickens as a model for the dreadful boarding school of 'Dotheboys Hall', which appears in Nicholas Nickleby (Plate 109). Both Sir Walter Scott and the artist Turner were inspired by Teesdale. Scott wrote his poem 'Rokeby' and Turner painted the famous Meeting of the Waters of the Rivers Tees and Greta. More local and less well-known, but still works of art in their own style, are the beautiful quilts embroidered by miners' wives and now seen in Beamish Museum (Plate 110).

The immense industrial energy of the Victorians, the tenfold growth in population and the reliance on only a few heavy basic industries contained the seeds of the County's later economic problems. The advent of oil-firing in ships and the loss of overseas markets for coal during the Great War of 1914-1918 saw the beginnings of a decline in the demand for coal. Not only that, many of the seams in the west of the County, mined for many centuries, were now worked out.

The early start in other industries also became a handicap as newer companies, both in Britain and abroad, equipped themselves with more modern machinery and competed in the world's markets. During the international trade slump of the 1920s and 30s, unemployment was particularly high in County Durham and North East England. Four out of every five men in Jarrow were unemployed and men in search of work marched from Jarrow to London in 1936. In those very difficult economic years, not enough was done to tackle the other Victorian legacies – the poor housing and the hideous industrial landscapes.

Despite the return to full employment during the Second World War, the inherent problems of the County's economy remained and had to be tackled. The County was changing rapidly and its dependence on the economy created by the Industrial Revolution diminished. Dozens of pits closed, leaving only a small number of collieries working the coal seams under the North Sea. The famous locomotive engineering works at Darlington (Plate 111) closed in the 1960s and the County's last major steelworks – at Consett – closed in 1980 (Plate 112). Jobs needed to be replaced, pit heaps to be reclaimed, new houses to be built, towns and villages to be improved. The next chapter deals with some of these changes.

83 Killhope Wheel was installed at the Park Level Mine in the late 19th Century to power the ore crushing rollers. It was an overshot wheel, 34 feet (10 metres) in diameter, driven by water from two reservoirs further up the hillside.

84 *Left* Evidence of Middleton in Teesdale's lead mining past can be seen in the school and houses built by the London Lead Mining Company and the fountain, a retirement memorial to the company's superintendent from the employees.

85 *Below* Middleton in Teesdale was a 'boom town' in the heyday of lead mining.

86 *Bottom* Park Level Mill at Killhope was built by the Blackett Beaumont Company.

87 *Far left* George Stephenson, who designed and built the first locomotive of the Stockton and Darlington Railway – 'Locomotion'.

88 *Centre left* Timothy Hackworth was the locomotive superintendent of the first public railway on the Stockton and Darlington Line.

89 *Left* Edward Pease was a Darlington businessman whose vision and business sense made the Stockton and Darlington Railway possible.

THE
STOCKTON & DARLINGTON
RAILWAY COMPANY
𝔥𝔢𝔯𝔢𝔟𝔶 𝔤𝔦𝔳𝔢 𝔑𝔬𝔱𝔦𝔠𝔢,

THAT the FORMAL OPENING of their RAILWAY will take place on the 27th instant, as announced in the public Papers.—The Proprietors will assemble at the Permanent Steam Engine, situated below BRUSSELTON TOWER*, *about nine Miles West of* DARLINGTON, *at 8 o'clock, and, after examining their extensive inclined Planes there, will start from the Foot of the* BRUSSELTON *descending Plane, at 9 o'clock, in the following Order :——*

1. THE COMPANY'S LOCOMOTIVE ENGINE.
2. The ENGINE'S TENDER, with Water and Coals.
3. SIX WAGGONS, laden with Coals, Merchandize, &c.
4. The COMMITTEE, and other PROPRIETORS, in the COACH belonging to the COMPANY.
5. SIX WAGGONS, with Seats reserved for STRANGERS.
6. FOURTEEN WAGGONS, for the Conveyance of Workmen and others.

☞ *The WHOLE of the above to proceed to* STOCKTON.

7. SIX WAGGONS, laden with Coals, to leave the Procession at the DARLINGTON BRANCH.
8. SIX WAGGONS, drawn by Horses, for Workmen and others.
9. Ditto   Ditto.
10. Ditto   Ditto.
11. Ditto   ·Ditto.

The COMPANY'S WORKMEN to leave the Procession at DARLINGTON, and DINE at that Place at ONE o'clock; excepting those to whom Tickets are specially given for YARM, and for whom Conveyances will be provided, on their Arrival at STOCKTON.

TICKETS will be given to the Workmen who are to dine at DARLINGTON, specifying the Houses of Entertainment.

The PROPRIETORS, and such of the NOBILITY and GENTRY as may honour them with their Company, will DINE precisely at THREE o'clock, at the TOWN-HALL, STOCKTON.—Such of the Party as may incline to return to DARLINGTON that Evening, will find Conveyances in waiting for their Accommodation, to start from the COMPANY'S WHARF there precisely at SEVEN o'clock.

The COMPANY take this Opportunity of enjoining on all their WORK-PEOPLE that Attention to *Sobriety* and *Decorum* which they have hitherto had the Pleasure of observing.

The COMMITTEE give this PUBLIC NOTICE, that all Persons who shall ride upon, or by the sides of, the RAILWAY, on Horseback, will incur the Penalties imposed by the Acts of Parliament passed relative to this RAILWAY.

* Any Individuals desirous of seeing the Train of Waggons descending the inclined Plane from ETHERLEY, and in Progress to BRUSSELTON, may have an Opportunity of so doing, by being on the RAILWAY at ST. HELEN'S AUCKLAND not later than Half-past Seven o'clock.

RAILWAY-OFFICE, *Sept.* 19th, 1825.

ATKINSON's Office, High-Row, Darlington.

93 *Above* The Market Hall
and clocktower at
Darlington.

94 Pease's House at
Darlington.

95 The first iron railway bridge was built near West Auckland, to carry the Stockton and Darlington Railway across the River Gaunless. Only two stone abutments can be seen at the site but the bridge was transported to York and is now on display in the National Railway Museum.

96 *Below* Hounsgill Viaduct near Consett was built in 1856.

97 *Right* The coal staithes at Seaham Harbour were opened in 1831. The port itself was part of Lord Londonderry's plan for a fine new town at Seaham but little of his original plan was ever built.

98 *Below* Waldridge Colliery was opened on 1st August 1831.
"On this occasion, a great number of the inhabitants of Chester le Street and neighbourhood assembled to witness the proceedings. About noon, the first waggon load of coals was drawn off amid the cheers of the populace, accompanied by a band of music." (*Local newspaper* 1831).

99 and 100 *Opposite* ▶ Consett Iron and Steel Works in the 19th Century. The giant blast furnaces dwarfed the town of 20,000 people (1860). Later, in 1952, Consett at night moved Sir Timothy Eden to write:
"*When the night falls, and the myriad little lights twinkle all over the countryside from villages suddenly grown beautiful in darkness, while the furnaces brandish their assegais, and the great iron works at Consett crowning all, tip up their regular recurring streams of fire – then one is almost tempted to be grateful to industry.*"

101 Thornley Colliery, photographed in 1970 after the closure of the mine, illustrates a once typical colliery scene with its waste heap, buildings and railway lines. Like most other collieries in the County the area has now been reclaimed and returned to agriculture and woodland.

102 A coal cutter in use in Beechburn Colliery during the 1920s.

103 The tipping of coal from the coastal pits despoiled some of the County's beaches. Although experiments on other methods of disposal are being carried out, tipping on the beaches still continues.

104 *Below* Colliery houses with unmade streets. Most have now disappeared.

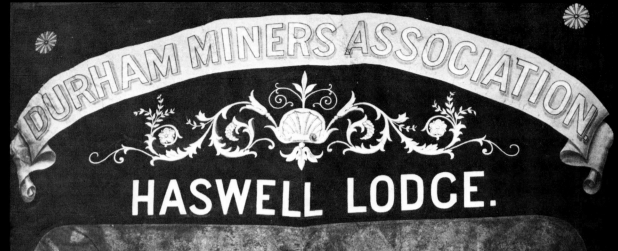

DURHAM MINERS ASSOCIATION.

HASWELL LODGE.

BUT TO ACT THAT EACH TO-MORROW
FINDS US FARTHER THAN TO-DAY.

105 An early lodge banner
of 1895 depicting the
contemporary leaders of
the Durham miners.

106 *Opposite above* ▶
A lodge banner with the
message that bereaved
miners' families could
look to the Union for
support.

107 *Opposite below* ▶
A 1930's lodge banner
depicting The Fable of the
Faggots. A child can break
a single stick but a strong
man is unable to break a
bundle of faggots bound
together for strength – an
illustration of the
combined strength of
Union membership.

108 The 'Big Meeting' at
Durham City in 1947.

109 'Dotheboys Hall' at Bowes, was the model for the infamous academy in Charles Dickens' Nicholas Nickleby.

110 Embroidered quilts made by miners' wives are exhibited at Beamish Museum. This one was made by Mrs. Stewart of Bowburn in about 1910.

111 A 'Peppercorn Pacific'
locomotive (No. 60147)
later named 'North
Eastern', photographed on
completion at the
Darlington North Road
Works in 1949.

COUNTY DURHAM TODAY
Living

13 Tunstall Reservoir
near Wolsingham.

Although the County of Durham made a big contribution to the growth of Britain as an industrial power, much of it is and always has been rural. Less than 6% of the County is covered with bricks and mortar, compared with 12% of England and Wales. The Pennine moors and dales in the west form a largely unspoiled rural area of great natural beauty. The south east of the County, too, is mainly farmland but the lower and flatter land there has a much gentler character than the western hills.

The thoughtless and greedy exploitation of Durham's mineral wealth was confined to the places under which the coal seams lay. There, the pit wheels turned in their hundreds and great heaps of pit stone were piled up alongside mean houses and shabby schools and shops. The Industrial Revolution did not, however, spawn any huge cities or industrial conurbations in the County. The biggest town – Darlington – has fewer than 90,000 residents and sits in pleasant countryside close to a lovely stretch of the River Tees. The next largest town – the City of Durham – is only half as big and you can, within minutes, walk along wooded river banks from the historic Market Place deep into fields and woods.

County Durham's miners had to endure harsh working conditions and even had to suffer being turned out of such poor homes as they had whenever they offended the mine owners. Their houses were overshadowed by smoking pit heaps or stood next to the colliery winding gear or the cokeworks but, almost everywhere, they lived within walking distance of green fields and open countryside. This rural setting was to be very important when the chance came to get rid of the despoliation and make the Durham coalfield a better place in which to live.

The need to do something about the problems inherited from the Victorians has been evident for long enough. In the 1920s and 30s many slums were pulled down, new schools were built and, even, trees were planted on one or two pit heaps, but the harsh economic climate of the depression years impeded any real progress. Indeed, the shortage of funds in those years made some of the problems worse – new buildings were built down to a price rather than up to a standard. There was no money for planting trees and shrubs to screen and soften the new buildings. It was only at the end of the Second World War that a real effort of improvement was made.

The County Council, in its first County Development Plan, set three broad aims:
   (i) to conserve and protect the unspoiled and attractive features of the County;
   (ii) to remove despoliation and dereliction;
   (iii) to improve the quality of life in the County.

The beauty of the County's landscape – not only in the west (Plates 113 to 115) but also in many places on the coalfield (Plate 116) – was not achieved by accident. It is the result of centuries of care by landowners and farmers. Unfortunately, since beauty is only skin deep, it is easily destroyed. Great care has to be taken to see that new buildings and other activities do not spoil the landscape and the things in it which we take so much for granted. Trees can be easily damaged and, like people, grow old and have to be replaced; hedges have to be maintained.

Similarly, many old villages and towns look attractive as a result of the care and craftsmanship of earlier generations. The buildings are simple and built of local materials. They look as though they belong. Care and imagination are needed to restore old buildings which have fallen into disrepair (Plates 117 and 118) and to fit new buildings into such a pleasant scene (Plate 133).

Given the enormous legacy of derelict land in the County, getting rid of eyesores has also required imagination and a lot of effort, too – 20 years of it – but with dramatic results. Towering black mountains have been replaced by green hillsides (Plates 119 to 126); trees planted on pit heaps are now 20 and 30 feet (6 and 9 metres) high and still growing; sheep and cattle graze and crops are grown where there were piles of pit stone. Old railways, disused industrial buildings and surplus army camps have disappeared – and not just one or two of them. Sixteen square miles (42 square kilometres) of derelict land have been restored – both in appearance and usefulness. Over 25 million tons of colliery and other wastes have been moved and more than 1¼ million trees have been planted. A start has been made on reclaiming the huge steelworks site at Consett and within two years there will be trees and grass growing on the old ironworks tip. The whole site should be just a memory within five years.

The effect of all this activity is obvious (or, perhaps, not so obvious!). It is now difficult to find, over a large part of what was a busy coalfield, any traces of coalmining. As the pits have gone, so have many of the pit workers' houses, to be replaced by new ones (Plates 127 to 132). Some of the better old houses have been improved, however, and so have their surroundings. The building of two new towns has provided opportunities for new and interesting house designs and neighbourhood layouts. Some have rightly won awards but others, perhaps inevitably, have been less successful.

Durham's towns are not so large and congested as to need 'out-of-town' shopping centres and a great deal of trouble has been taken to fit new shops in with the old (Plates 135 and 136). Shopping has also been made more pleasant by the removal of traffic from most of the County's main shopping streets (Plates 134 and 137).

Many of the old cramped schools in which children were not expected to do more than learn the three 'Rs' and then go down the pit have been replaced (Plate 139). A far wider range of interests and activities (Plates 138 and 140) is now provided for, giving opportunities for children to go on from school to colleges of further education (Plate 142) and to University. Durham University is England's third oldest and has many attractive buildings (Plates 141, 143 and 144).

114 Farmland in the west of the County.

115 *Above* The moors above St. John's Chapel in Weardale.

116 Landscape of the Durham Coalfield near Pittington.

117 Weavers' cottages in Thorngate, Barnard Castle, restored by the Teesdale Buildings Preservation Trust.

118 West Auckland Manor House restored by the owner.

119 and 120 These houses at Sherburn Hill now overlook open fields instead of towering black pit heaps.

121 and 122 The removal of the pit heap at Roddymoor together with other improvements brought about a big change in the appearance of the area.

123 and 124 *Below and right* From mineral extraction to food production; an impressive transformation following careful reclamation work at Thornley Colliery.

125 and 126 *Above and right* More and more land in the County is being freed for new uses. In 1969 few could imagine that this grubby derelict site at Bowden Close, near Willington, would soon be covered by green fairways.

127-129 New and
imaginative housing
schemes by local
authorities and housing
associations are helping to
provide new homes in
many of the County's
towns and villages.

127 *Right* Cobbler's Hall,
Newton Aycliffe.

128 *Far right* Henknowle,
Bishop Auckland.

129 *Centre* Staindrop.

130-132 Modern private
housing offers a wide
variety of styles from
terraced town houses to
large spacious detached
properties.

130 *Left* Aycliffe Village.

131 *Below* Darlington.

132 *Right* Durham City.

133 *Above* New houses, designed to fit in with their surroundings, fill in gaps in existing villages like Easington.

134 The removal of traffic from Stanley Front Street provides safe and pleasant shopping.

135 and 136 Millburngate
Shopping Centre in
Durham City has been
sympathetically designed
to merge with the historic
townscape; inside, it
provides modern shops.

137 *Left* Traffic-free
shopping in Durham City.
The scheme to remove
vehicles from the City's
mediaeval streets has been
highly acclaimed.

138 *Below* A pottery class
at Framwellgate Moor
Comprehensive School.

139 *Bottom* Peases West
County Junior and Infants
School, Crook.

140 Outdoor activities at the field centre in Ireshopeburn in Weardale.

141 Congregation Procession following a degree ceremony in Durham Castle.

142 Drama class at New College, Durham City.

143 Abbey House, on Palace Green, is now used by the University's Department of Theology.

144 *Opposite* One of the ▶ many modern buildings at Durham University, Van Mildert College.

COUNTY DURHAM TODAY Working

45 New factories on
modern industrial estates
help to attract new jobs to
the County – a nursery
unit at Newton Aycliffe.

The 'coal-rush' of the 19th Century did not just affect the appearance of the towns and villages of Durham; it decided what a lot of people did for a living. They either went down the pits or into the steelworks or shipyards. There was little other choice.

Worse still, not only were people very dependent on this extremely limited range of jobs, these industries were, in turn, very dependent on each other. If the demand for ships slackened, so did the orders for steel plate, and the demand for coal and coke. So, when trade slumped in the 1920s and 30s whole communities were thrown out of work in Jarrow and many other places like it. The County suffered terribly from unemployment between the two world wars.

The demands of the Second World War brought back full employment for a time but it became quite obvious that some of Durham's traditional industries could not go on providing jobs. So far as coalmining was concerned, it was not only a question of economics or competition. The seams of coal in the west of the County had been worked for so many hundreds of years that much of the best coal had gone. With no coal coming from local pits, the coke and by-products works could not continue. Even major steelworks had to import oil to fuel their furnaces. Changes had to come in the County's economy – in the things people do for a living – and they came quickly.

Twenty-five years ago, three Durham workers in five were still employed in the heavy industries – coalmining, chemicals, steelmaking, heavy engineering. Few women went out to work. Many of the once traditional and familiar jobs have now completely disappeared. A vigorous programme of industrial building and promotion by central and local government has provided a much wider range of better jobs for both men and women in modern factories and offices.

The oldest industry of all, farming, is still well in evidence (Plate 146) since it occupies 86% of the County's land surface even though it does not provide as many jobs as it used to. The modern equipment (Plate 147) and buildings found on many farms in the central and southern lowlands help fewer hands to produce more food. New farming techniques are taught at the Agricultural College at Houghall, near Durham City (Plate 148). In the dales, the scene may appear little changed but careful sheep breeding is continuing to produce some of the finest animals in the country.

Coalmining is perhaps the industry for which the County was best known but it, too, is no longer a major provider of jobs. There are now only 10 active collieries where 25 years ago there used to be over 100. Production is centred on five big coastal pits where coal seams are worked up to five miles (8 kilometres) out under the North Sea (Plate 150).

The closure of collieries in the rest of the County is not, however, the end of the story of 'King Coal'. Some of the coal which the old-time miners left behind is now being dug out by surface mining (Plate 149). Although these sites can be scars on the landscape while they are working, most of them are usually well restored afterwards and all traces of the workings are hidden beneath new fields and woodland. Only the new and straighter fences tell the tale until the newly planted hedges grow.

Like the old coal seams, old lead veins are also being re-worked (Plate 152). This time it is for fluorspar – once regarded as waste by the lead miners. The attractive fluorspar crystals (Plate 151) are now an important raw material in many manufacturing processes – helping to make refrigerators, aerosols, glass and enamels.

Limestone is still quarried in Weardale as it has been for many years and the cement works at Eastgate, one of the landmarks in the dale, is a major local employer. Further east, the Magnesian limestone is quarried at Thrislington, Raisby and Cornforth for use in the iron and steel, chemical and refractory industries.

New industries on modern industrial estates (Plates 145 and 153) provide jobs to replace those lost in coalmining and the other basic industries. Factories vary in size from small nursery units (Plate 155) in which new businesses can find their feet (Plate 154), to the giant factories of established international names like Black and Decker, Ever Ready (Berec), Coca Cola and Mullard (Plate 156).

The County's two new towns, Peterlee and Newton Aycliffe have helped to attract new firms (Flymo, N.S.K. Bearings (Europe), Fisher Price and Electrolux among them) as well as providing smaller modern factory buildings (Plate 157).

In emphasising the new face of industry in the County, it is important, however, not to forget older but still well-known faces. The Cleveland Bridge and Engineering Company was established in Darlington in 1877 and since then has gained a world-wide reputation for bridge building, being associated with the Victoria Falls Bridge, the Severn and Forth road bridges, the bridge over the

Bosphorus, linking Europe with Asia and, most recently, the Humber Bridge.

The Wolsingham Steel Company has managed to survive the recession in the iron and steel industry by specialising in high integrity casting. Located in a quiet dales town, it has made the rudders for some of the Navy's most famous ships – the Ark Royal, the Illustrious and the Invincible. It also made part of the anchor for the QE2. An international reputation has also been gained by two Durham City firms – Hugh Mackay, for high quality carpets (Plate 159), and Harrison and Harrison, the organ builders, who have been making fine instruments for over 100 years, including the organs in Durham Cathedral, Coventry Cathedral, St. Albans Abbey and the Royal Festival Hall (Plate 158).

Overall, the County today makes everything from heavy metal goods, chemicals, plastics and car components to toys, refrigerators, soft drinks, micro-processors, antibiotics (Plate 161) and cigarettes.

Contrary to the popular image of County Durham, however, the largest industrial sector in terms of jobs is the service sector. Durham City is a major service centre with three large employers: the County Council, housed in a modern County Hall to the north of the city centre (Plate 160); part of the Department of National Savings, in a modern office block overlooking the river; and the University.

Some of the success in revitalising the County's economy can be attributed to the improvements made to the County's communications network. There is an excellent road system based on the A.1 Motorway (Plate 162) and high speed trains provide quick transport to London, the Midlands, South West England and Scotland (Plate 163).

Two local airports, at Teesside and Newcastle, provide links to London and Europe, and by sea there are passenger and cargo services from Tyneside and Teesport.

The County's economy has undoubtedly improved but not enough has yet been done to replace all the lost jobs and the County's longstanding economic problems have been further aggravated by recent steelworks' closures.

146 and 147 Farming in County Durham. *Above* at White Cross Farm, near Piercebridge. *Below* one of the modern milking parlours which can be found on farms throughout the County.

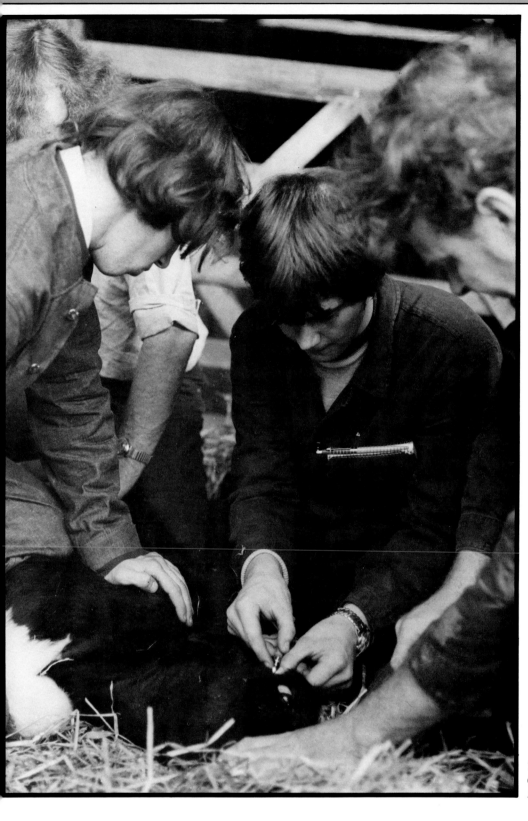

148 Learning to de-horn calves at Houghall Agricultural College.

149 Opencast coal mining.

150 *Below* Working on the coal face three miles (five kilometres) out under the sea at Dawdon Colliery, one of Europe's most technically advanced coal mines.

151 Fluorspar crystals.

152 *Below* Fluorspar mining in Weardale has revived an interest in the old lead mines.

153 One of the new industrial estates in the County at Peterlee New Town.

155 A terrace of small nursery units built by the County Council at Chilton.

154 Ampion – a micro processor company – set up business in a nursery unit at Tanfield Lea near Stanley.

156 Mullard Ltd., part of the Dutch company Philips, built a large factory at Belmont near Durham City.

157 Modern factory buildings in Newton Aycliffe and Peterlee New Towns.

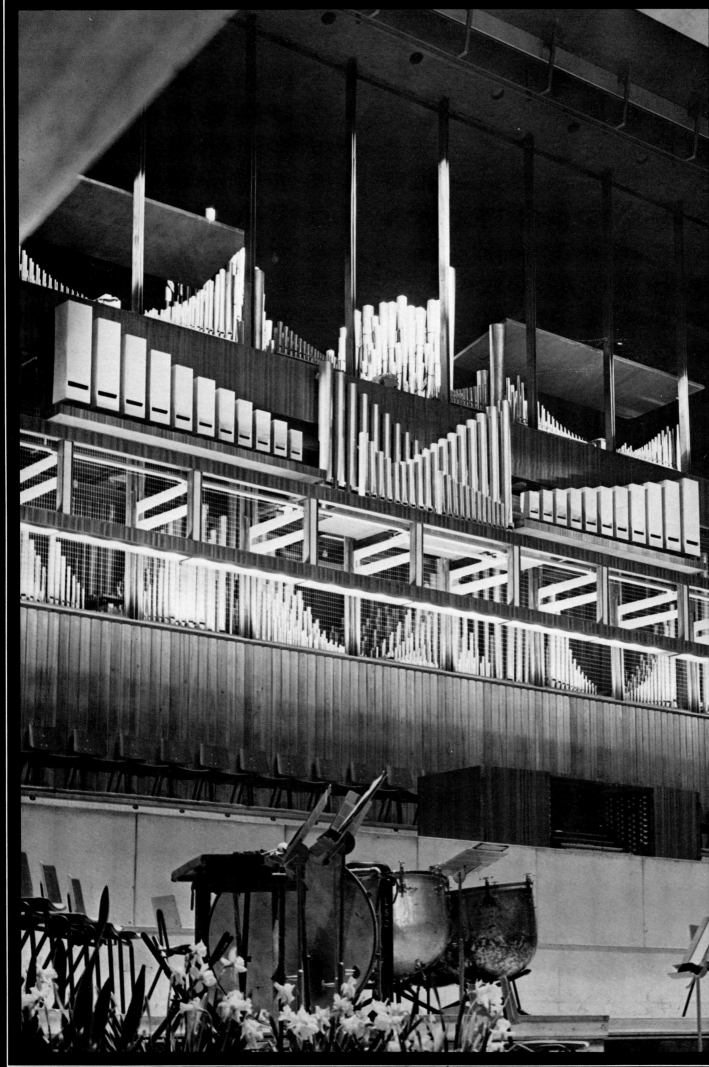

158 *Opposite* The organ built by Harrison and Harrison Ltd., of Durham City, for the Royal Festival Hall.

159 *Below* Strands of wool going into the carpet loom at Hugh Mackay Ltd., Durham City.

160 *Above* County Hall is situated in Durham City which is the administrative centre for the County.

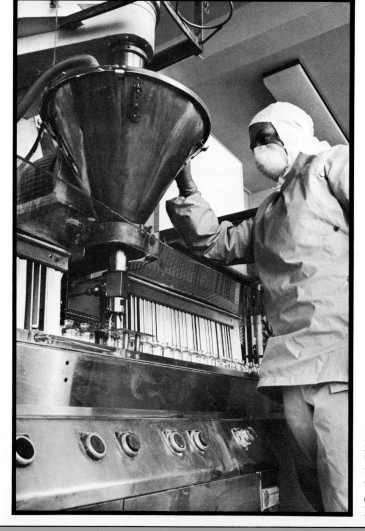

161 A fully gowned and masked girl operator fills bottles for antibiotics under sterile conditions at the Barnard Castle factory of Glaxo Operations UK Ltd.

162 An interchange on the
A1(M) at Chester le Street.

163 A High Speed Train
on its way to London.

COUNTY DURHAM TODAY Leisure

64 Bowlees Picnic Area, west of Middleton in Teesdale. Here visitors can wander along beside the stream or around the visitor centre which explains the life in Upper Teesdale and its plants and animals.

Despite the great changes in the County in recent years, many traditional leisure-time activities still flourish. The working men's clubs, originally formed and financed by workers to avoid paying their wages to the big brewers, are still very popular and their 'Federation' beer has even found its way into the Houses of Parliament! After long dark hours in the pits, men sought pleasure in the open air. Prize leek and chrysanthemum growing (Plate 165), pigeon and whippet racing (Plates 166 to 168), have all kept their popularity if the number of leek shows held each September and of brightly painted pigeon 'crees' in village allotments are anything to go by.

Brass bands were also strongly associated with colliery life. Each colliery had its own band which played the union lodge banner into the annual 'big meeting' of pitmen in Durham City. As the pits closed, some of the well known bands disappeared but others live on sponsored by new firms. Examples include the nationally famous Ever Ready (Berec) Band, which was the Craghead Colliery Band, the Amoco Band and the National Smokeless Fuels Band, formerly the Fishburn Colliery Band (Plate 169), all of which do well in the national brass band championships.

Not all traditional pastimes are associated with mining villages. The countryside had, and still has, its own particular sports. Quoits pits can still be seen in some of the Teesdale villages and Sedgefield has a very distinctive sport – the Ball Game. Held each Shrove Tuesday, the game originated over 900 years ago as a competition between local farmers and traders, and has been described by some as dangerous and barbarous. Whoever scores the goal is allowed to keep the ball, but he is a lucky man if he returns home unscathed.

Other longstanding sporting traditions include rowing, steeplechasing and cricket. Durham Regatta (Plate 171) founded in 1834 is England's oldest rowing regatta. There was horse racing at Sedgefield in 1732 and the County's first steeplechase was held there in 1846 in the grounds of Sands Hall near the present course (Plate 170). Durham is also proud of its cricketing tradition (Plate 172). The County Club was formed in 1882 and was one of the joint winners of the first Minor Counties Championship in 1895. Since then, Durham has won on seven subsequent occasions including 1980 and 1981.

Football, rugby (Plate 173), and bowls are enjoyed in most towns and villages. The County has known many past glories in amateur football. In 1910 and 1911 West Auckland won the first World Cup in Italy, beating the mighty Stuttgart and Juventus! Teams have won the Amateur Cup at Wembley (Plate 174) on many occasions and in the late 50s and 60s Bishop Auckland won the Cup ten times. There is only one professional club – Darlington – but avid fans need not travel far to watch Sunderland, Middlesbrough, Hartlepool and the 'Magpies' at Newcastle.

New sports centres have greatly extended the range and season of energetic activities – hockey, five-a-side football, squash, table tennis, the martial arts and fitness training (Plates 175 to 177). Modern well-equipped swimming pools provide hours of enjoyment (Plate 178).

All the usual outdoor pursuits (Plates 179 to 182) can be enjoyed around the County. In the countryside, horse riding, pony trekking, orienteering, canoeing on the white water of the Tees, hunting, beagling and rough shooting all have their ardent followers. In winter, cross-country and Alpine skiing are attractions on the slopes of Weardale and Teesdale. Angling is popular in the County's rivers and reservoirs (Plate 183). For those who prefer sea fishing, there is the foreshore along the coast and the sea-wall at Seaham. Some of the reservoirs high up in the dales are used for rowing, sailing and water-skiing (Plates 184 and 185).

Walking is also popular – from a quiet stroll along riverbanks to long distance walks like the Pennine Way, which crosses the western part of the County (Plates 186 and 187), and the lesser known Wear Valley Way 46 miles (74 kilometres). In addition to these, over 34 miles (55 kilometres) of old railways have been converted by the County Council into moorland walks, shady footpaths, cycle tracks and bridleways (Plate 188). These include the Waskerley Way, which crosses over the moors from Consett towards Stanhope, and the Derwent Walk, which winds up the wooded Derwent Valley. As well as these walks, the restoration of some of the coal-stained beaches has improved the chance of a seaside stroll (Plates 189 and 190).

Many people prefer short walks after a drive into the countryside, and country parks, picnic sites, footpaths and forest trails have been created. Picnic sites provide convenient stopping places for those on long journeys or allow people to visit points of local interest like the waterfalls at Bowlees (Plates

164 and 194), Killhope Wheel (Plate 83) and Causey Arch (Plate 82). Hardwick Hall Country Park, in a former 18th Century landscaped garden, now provides a pleasant spot to walk or sit while the children sail model boats or fish for minnows in the lake and explore the nature trail (Plates 191 to 193).

Other people make for the picturesque villages in Weardale and Teesdale. A number of these villages hold annual shows where you can see sheep dog trials and stock judging. You can also wander through tents crammed with bright chrysanthemums, begonias, enormous onions and plump tomatoes; or amongst tempting stalls full of jams and cakes; and enjoy the excitement of the gymkhana and sulky racing (Plates 195 and 196).

A wide variety of plays, operas and concerts is staged by local and national companies. The Royal Shakespeare Company have made Newcastle their third home and local theatres have regular visits from the Scottish Opera, Royal Ballet and Ballet Rambert. The one remaining theatre in the County, the former Hippodrome in Darlington, was opened in 1907 (Plate 197). As the Darlington Civic Theatre, it still attracts well known artists. Music lovers can hear concerts throughout the year by the Northern Sinfonia of England Orchestra and many world famous musicians attend the annual music festivals held in Durham City and Newcastle.

Arts Centres in Durham City (Plate 198), Peterlee and Darlington stage an exciting variety of activities from classical recitals and jazz concerts, to craft workshops and exhibitions. Folk music thrives in many of the County's pubs and regular ceilidhs are held in Durham Town Hall.

For those wanting to know more about the County's past or about arts and culture abroad, County Durham is particularly rich in museums. The Gulbenkian Museum of Oriental Art in Durham City houses a unique collection of Chinese, Japanese, Egyptian and Tibetan art, sculptures and porcelain in an impressive modern building (Plates 200 and 201). Durham City can also boast three other museums; the Old Fulling Mill Museum of Archaeology in a picturesque setting beside the River Wear; the Cathedral Treasury Museum and Monk's Dormitory in Durham Cathedral which contain relics of St. Cuthbert, magnificent silver plate and some beautiful illuminated manuscripts; and the Durham Light Infantry Museum which proudly displays military vehicles, drums (Plate 199) and medals won by the County's 'Faithful Durhams'. The Regiment traces its birth back to

1758 and its first colonel was General John Lambton of Lambton Castle. It was given the motto 'Faithful' for its services in the West Indies.

The Bowes Museum, a grand 'French chateau' is an unexpected sight in the market town of Barnard Castle. This magnificent edifice was built in 1869 by John and Josephine Bowes to house their impressive collection of European art, porcelain and furniture. In addition to a fine array of paintings, including Goyas, Canalettos and an El Greco, there is an exhibition tracing the history of life in the dales and a delightful costume gallery (Plates 202 to 205).

The North of England Open Air Museum at Beamish provides an opportunity to relive some of the North East's history. It is possible to ride on an old Gateshead tramcar; watch bread being baked in a coal-fired oven; see locomotives steaming into Rowley Station; go underground into a genuine coal drift mine; travel in style in a horse-drawn carriage (Plates 206 to 209); and relax in the cafe or enjoy a pint in the Bobby Shafto pub.

One particular aspect of Durham's history – the birth of the railways – is commemorated in two specialist museums. Darlington Railway Museum is in the original North Road passenger station on the Stockton and Darlington railway line. It illustrates the history of the railway and its showpiece is the original 'Locomotion' built by George Stephenson. The Shildon home and engineering works of Timothy Hackworth, another great railway pioneer, have also been converted into a museum. The house contains exhibits from the times of this great 19th Century inventor and, in the Soho Engine Works, there stands a working replica of the 'Sanspareil' which competed in the Rainhill Locomotive Trials in 1829.

Many British and foreign tourists are attracted to these museums each year and County Durham has a lot more to offer with its own fine scenery and proximity to the beautiful unspoilt beaches of Northumberland and no less than four National Parks – the Lake District, Yorkshire Dales, North York Moors and Northumberland. Visitors can stay in a variety of accommodation – camping and caravan sites, hotels, country cottages, university colleges and village pubs (Plates 210 and 211). A tour of these pubs may, in itself, prove to be a good way of finding out about the County since its history – factual and legendary – is illustrated in their colourful signs (Plate 212).

166 Whippet breeding is also popular. Here, Dan Armstrong of Craghead proudly exhibits *Thurma Royal Event*, winner of the open whippet section of the Durham County Show in 1981.

167 *Don Quijote*, a National Whippet Racing Champion (1977) owned by Mrs. D. Cairns of Brandon.

165 *Opposite* Each year, members of the local clubs coax and guard jealously their prize leeks until they are ready to be displayed proudly at the annual leek show.

168 Pigeon fancying,
another traditional
pastime of the mining
villages.

169 The Fishburn Colliery Band after winning a National Coal Board Competition in 1968. The band is now sponsored by National Smokeless Fuels.

170 *Above* National Hunt racing at Sedgefield. The County's first steeplechase was held in 1846 near to the present course.

171 Durham Regatta is England's oldest rowing event. It is claimed that the regatta was founded in 1815 to celebrate the Battle of Waterloo, but the first authentic record is 1834.

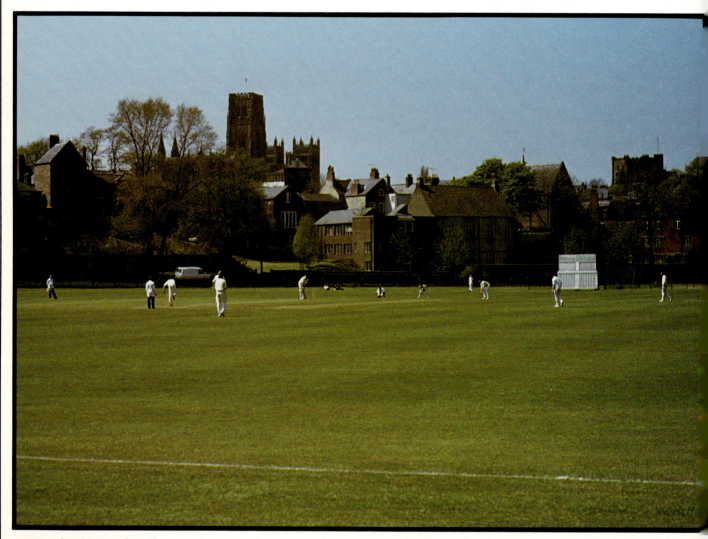

172 Cricket being played
on the University ground
in Durham City.

173 Rugby Football is played throughout the County.

174 *Below* Bishop Auckland celebrate their Amateur Cup win at Wembley in 1955.

175-177 Indoor sports in modern sports centres at Spennymoor, Consett and Newton Aycliffe.

178 Swimming pool at Chester le Street. One of the County's many modern pools.

179 *Right* and 181 *Bottom*
Each year groups of
international sportsmen
race through the County –
on two wheels in the Milk
Race and on four wheels in
the RAC Rally.

180 *Above* Golf on the
course beside Brancepeth
Castle.

182 *Far right* Skiing in
Weardale.

184 Sailing on Derwent Reservoir in North West Durham.

183 *Opposite* Fishing on the River Wear, a more tranquil pursuit rewarded by good catches of trout.

185 Water skiing on Balderhead Reservoir.

186 Walkers on the Pennine Way, a 250 mile (400 kilometres) walk which passes through Teesdale en route from the Peak District of Derbyshire to the Scottish Border.

187 *Below* The Pennine Way follows the valley of the River Tees alongside Falcon Clints.

188 The Deerness Valley Walk, once part of the railway passenger line to Esh Winning and Waterhouses.

189 and 190 *Opposite* The coastline near Crimdon before and after reclamation. *Above* begrimed by coal dust, and *below* restored to golden sand.

191 Hardwick Hall Country Park, part of a former beautifully landscaped garden created in the 18th Century by John Burdon. It is now equipped with picnic tables overlooking the lake, a nature trail and landing stages for fishing or sailing model boats.

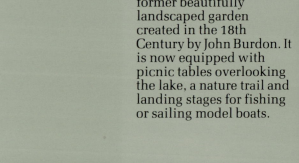

192 In the 18th Century the lake was said to be 'the finest sheet of water in the North of England' and was surrounded by temples, statues and grottoes. Today the area of water is much reduced but the lakeside paths are still extremely pleasant for a stroll.

193 The Boardwalk Nature Trail. Even those not interested in wildlife enjoy exploring the boardwalk through the lush vegetation.

194 Gibson's Cave waterfall at Bowlees.

195 and 196 The annual Stanhope Show, a traditional country event.

195 Sulky racing.

196 Judging the famous Weardale mule sheep which are a cross between blue faced Leicester rams and hardy Swaledale ewes.

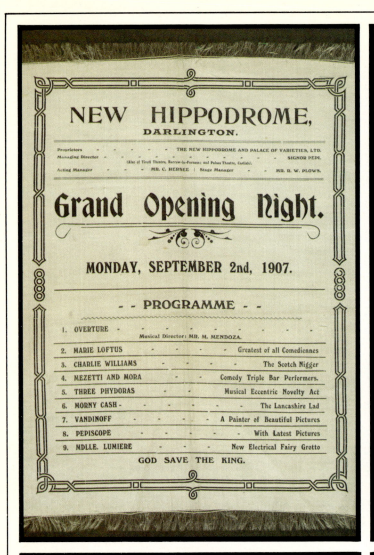

NEW HIPPODROME,
DARLINGTON.

Proprietors	THE NEW HIPPODROME AND PALACE OF VARIETIES, LTD.
Managing Director	SIGNOR PEPI.
	(Also of Tivoli Theatre, Barrow-in-Furness; and Palace Theatre, Carlisle).
Acting Manager	MR. C. HERSEE	Stage Manager	MR. D. W. PLOWS.

Grand Opening Night.

MONDAY, SEPTEMBER 2nd, 1907.

-- PROGRAMME --

Musical Director: MR. M. MENDOZA.

1. OVERTURE -
2. MARIE LOFTUS - Greatest of all Comediennes
3. CHARLIE WILLIAMS - The Scotch Nigger
4. MEZETTI AND MORA - Comedy Triple Bar Performers.
5. THREE PHYDORAS - Musical Eccentric Novelty Act
6. MORNY CASH - The Lancashire Lad
7. VANDINOFF - A Painter of Beautiful Pictures
8. PEPISCOPE - With Latest Pictures
9. MDLLE. LUMIERE - New Electrical Fairy Grotto

GOD SAVE THE KING.

THE HIPPODROME, Darlington

FLYING MATINEE ONLY

THURSDAY, NOVEMBER 17th, at 2.30 p.m.

EDMUND RUSSON has
the honour to present

PAVLOVA

supported by

LAURENT NOVIKOFF

Corps de Ballet

And CONTINGENT OF

COVENT GARDEN ORCHESTRA

Conductor - WALFORD HYDEN

Prices : Reserved Seats, Fauteuils and Dress Circle, 10/6 ;
Orchestra Stalls and Circle, 7/6 ; Unreserved, Pit
Stalls, 5/9 ; Gallery, 2/4

Plan & Tickets at Richmond's Box Office, Park Gate
'Phone: 2306 Darlington

BOX OFFICE NOW OPEN

DARLINGTON CIVIC THEATRE

Theatre Director: PETER TOD   Box Office open daily from 10 a.m. to 8.30 p.m. Telephone 65774
MONDAY, 6th DECEMBER, until SATURDAY, 11th DECEMBER, one week only
Nightly at 7.30 p.m.   Matinees Wednesday and Friday at 2.30 p.m.   Tickets £1.60, £1.40, £1.20 and £1.00
Generous Party Booking Concessions for all performances. O.A.P. concessions on Monday and Tuesday evenings.
Children and Students £1.00 at all performances except Friday and Saturday evenings.

DUNCAN C WELDON and LOUIS I MICHAELS
for Triumph Theatre (Productions) Ltd. and
The Yvonne Arnaud Theatre Guildford
PRESENT

PAUL **Daneman**	DOROTHY **Tutin**
PAUL **Curran**	EDGAR **Wreford**
MALCOLM **Stoddard**	ROBIN **Wentworth**

in

Macbeth

by William Shakespeare

WITH

Chris Channer · Ellen Cullen · Peter Davidson
Michael Fawkes · Caroline High · Jon Iles
Paul Large · James Leith · Robert Lister
Annette Lynton · Charles Rogers · Sarah Ross
Vivienne Ross · James Rowe · Ray Skipp
AND
Richard Owens

Directed by PETER COE

Designed by Michael Knight
Lighting by Mick Hughes
Fight Director William Hobbs

197 *Opposite* Darlington Civic Theatre — a mixture of old and new bills. The bill for the performance by Pavlova is very special in the history of the theatre. It was the dream of the theatre's Italian Manager, Signor Pepi, to have Pavlova dance in his theatre. She eventually agreed to give one matinee performance in 1927 but unfortunately Signor Pepi never saw his dream come true – he died on that very afternoon.

198 The Durham Light Infantry Museum and Arts Centre.

199 A permanent exhibition of uniforms, drums and military vehicles belonging to the DLI regiment.

200 and 201 Exhibits at the Gulbenkian Museum in Durham City.

200 Egyptian Statue of Meriptah, High Priest of Amun dated 1380 B.C.

201 Earthenware model of horse from the T'ang Dynasty (618-906 A.D.).

202 The Bowes Museum was built by John and Josephine Bowes but it only opened to the public in 1892 after their deaths. The building itself is in grand French style and the collections of paintings, porcelain and furniture are of international repute.

203 *Below The Tears of St. Peter* by El Greco (1541-1614).

204 *Centre right* A 1920's doll's house.

205 *Bottom right* The famous silver swan.

206-209 Scenes from Durham's past reconstructed at the North of England Open Air Museum at Beamish, opened in 1971.

206 Steam tractor at Home Farm.

207 Baking bread in a pit cottage.

208 A re-creation of a typical colliery of about 1913.

209 Rowley Station built in 1867 was brought to Beamish from a village in the hills beyond Consett.

210 The Europa Lodge
Hotel at Darlington,
originally Blackwell
Grange which had been
the home of Sir Henry
Havelock-Allan.

211 The Rose and Crown
Inn at Romaldkirk.

212   Pub signs.

THE EDEN ARMS

SI·SIT·PRUDENTIA

Samuel Smith

ELDON ARMS

DURHAM 5

Kicking Cuddy

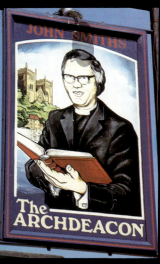

JOHN SMITHS

The
ARCHDEACON

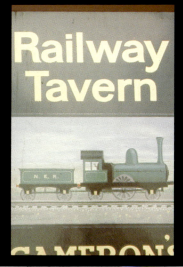

Railway
Tavern

ACKNOWLEDGEMENTS

The County Planning Officer would like to thank Jeanne Bateson, Ken Frankish and Ian Woods of the County Planning Department for their very considerable assistance in the preparation of the book and all the others who provided information, comments and photographs. All photographs, apart from those listed below, belong to Durham County Council.

Agricultural Development and Advisory Service, Ministry of Agriculture, Fisheries and Food 147
Beamish: North of England Open Air Museum 61, 75, 99, 110, 207, 208, 209
The Bowes Museum 203, 204, 205
John Burles 173, 177
Mrs. D. Cairns 167
The Civic Trust 137
Ursula Clark 9, 14, 28, 30, 48, 49, 62, 63, 66, 69, 70, 72, 73, 74, 80, 96
Borough of Darlington 93, 94
Darlington Civic Theatre 197
The Dean and Chapter of Durham 25, 29, 38, 39, 40, 41
Ian Dobson 166
City of Durham Council 135
Fox Photos Ltd. for Harrison & Harrison Ltd. 158
Keith Gibson 136
Glaxo Operations U.K. Ltd. 161
Dr. P. Holmes 91
M. J. Hudson of the Nature Conservancy Council 17, 18, 19
John Hunt 178
M. Leatherland 185
W. A. Moyes 105, 106, 107, 108
National Coal Board 150
National Coal Board Opencast Executive 149
Newcastle Chronicle and Journal Ltd. 112
North of England Development Council 6
North of England Newspapers 174
Peterlee Development Corporation 153
Pitkin Pictorials Ltd. 37
T. Ruecroft 169
Sedgefield District Council 175, 176
South Tyneside Public Libraries and Museums 102
Swiss Aluminium Mining (U.K.) Ltd. 151, 152
Royston Thomas 132
University of Durham 34, 141, 172
University of Newcastle upon Tyne 97
Wear Valley District Council 81
Peter Wilson 111
W. M. Wilson 182
Ian R. J. Woods 10, 52, 58, 67, 95, 163, 171

FURTHER READING

Allsop, B. ed. Modern architecture of Northern England. 1969.

Atkinson, F. Life and tradition in Northumberland and Durham. 1977.

Atkinson, F. Industrial archaeology of North East England. 2 vols. 1974.

Baker, A. R. H. and J. B. Harley. eds. Man made the land: essays in English historical geography. 1973.

Berryman, B. Durham. 2nd ed. 1969.

Billings, R. W. Illustrations of the architectural antiquities of the County of Durham. Facsimile reprint. 1974.

Blair, P. H. Northumbria in the days of Bede. 1976.

Bulmer, M. ed. Mining and social change: Durham County in the twentieth Century. 1978.

Central Office of Information In Review: an introduction to the Northern Region. 1976.

Chapman, V. Rural Darlington. 1975.

Chapman, V. Rural Durham. 1977.

Clack, P. A. G. and P. F. Gosling Archaeology in the North. 1976.

Clapham, A. R. ed. Upper Teesdale: the area and its natural history. 1978.

Daniels, P., Hewitt, D., Cowey, D. J. and G. Flynn Railway People. 1975.

Dewdney, J. C. ed. Durham County and City with Teesside. 1970.

Durham County Library Castles of County Durham. 1979. Darlington. 1975. Durham City. 1975. (Three sets of reproduction prints).

Eden, Sir T. C. Durham. 2 vols. 1952.

Fordyce, W. A history of coal, coke and coalfields . . . iron, its ores and process of manufacture . . . 1860.

Fynes, R. The Miners of Northumberland and Durham. 1971.

Garside, W. R. The Durham Miners, 1919-1960. 1971.

Gibby, C. W. A short history of Durham City. 1972.

Hair, T. H. Sketches of the coalmines in Northumberland and Durham. 1839.

Institute of Geological Sciences Geology of the country around Barnard Castle. 1976.

Institute of Geological Sciences Geology of the country between Durham and West Hartlepool. 1967.

Johnson, M. Durham City: a pictorial history. 2nd ed. 1974.

Jones, H. and W. B. Fisher Durham City. 1976.

McCord, N. North East England: the region's development 1760-1960. 1979.

McDougall, C. A. The Stockton and Darlington Railway. 2nd ed. 1975.

Moyes, W. A. The Banner Book: the study of the banners of the lodges of Durham Miners' Association. 1974.

Nelson, I. Durham City as it was. 1977.

Parker, M. Discovery Guide Series to: Durham City and County. 1980; Teesdale. 1981; Weardale, Allendale, South Tynedale. 1979.

Parker, M. Stories, sketches and places to visit in Teesdale. 1980. Stories, sketches and places to visit in Durham. 1980.

Pevsner, N. The buildings of England, County Durham. 1953.

Pevsner, N. The buildings of England, Yorkshire the North Riding. 1966.

Pocock, D. C. D. Durham: Images of a Cathedral City. 1975.

Roberts, B. K. The green villages of County Durham. 1977.

Rowland, T. H. Dere Street, Roman Road North. 1974.

Rushford, F. H. This is Durham. 1964.

Smailes, A. E. North England. 1968.

Spedding, T. R. Walking in Weardale. 1974.

Tegner, H. S. Natural history in Northumberland and Durham. 1972.

Thomas, D., St. J. and C. R. Clinker, eds. A regional history of the railways of Great Britain: vol. 4. North East England, by K. Hoole. 1978.

Thompson, H. Durham Villages. 1976.

Thorold, H. County Durham. 1980.

Tomlinson, W. W. The North Eastern Railway. 2nd ed. 1967.

Turnbull, L. The history of lead mining in the North East of England. 1975.

White, P. A. Portrait of County Durham. 2nd ed. 1976.

Whittaker, N. The house and cottage handbook. 1976.

Whittaker, N. The old halls and manor houses of Durham. 1975.

Whittaker, N. and U. V. Clark Historic architecture of County Durham. 1971.

Wilcock, D. The Durham Coalfield: Part 1. The 'Sea Coal Age'. 1979.

Wilkinson, A. Twenty family walks: interesting and short walks in historic Teesdale's beautiful scenery. 1978.

A selection of further references is given in:
Durham County Library Books of Local Interest. 1982.